KULAL'S SHADOW

PAUL MEYER

Wrensong Books
Seattle, Washington

WRENSONG

KULAL'S SHADOW

For Information, address
Wrensong Books
4900 S. Hudson Seattle WA 98118
e-mail paulmeyer@seanet.com

Printing History
First Printing 2001
Library of Congress Control Number: 2001087339
ISBN : 0-9707441-0-2

Printed in the United States of America
10 9 8 7 9 5 7 3 2

Chalbi Desert Region of Kenya

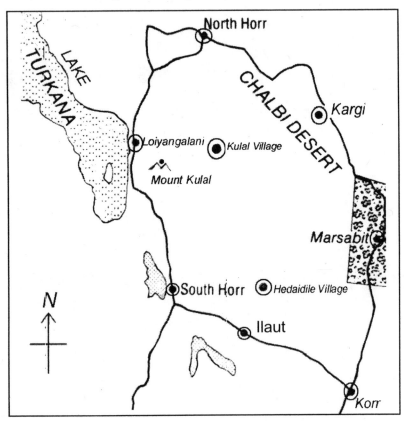

Two hours after sunset, the heat of the desert still burned at Firingin's sandals.

He took no notice. The police would return, and he must be far from this place before their searching eyes came looking.

He scanned toward the constellations that swarmed the canopy and ahead to the beacon-star on the horizon, the star of the North. He would use that star's light to guide him to the Chalbi Desert. Across its cindered plain he would travel to a country unknown, a new home for his wife and for the child she carried inside her body.

A gust of wind blew from the west and filled the air with a thick and penetrating grit. The young camel at the rear of the column snorted, and Firingin looked back. His eyes stopped on his wife. Atop the old camel in front, Leslie appeared to be asleep. Firingin smiled. It was good that she rested. She would need to remain strong for the trip they must now make.

He leaned into the rising wind and thought of the parting from his Grandfather Jeiso.

The head elder of the desert community played at bau when Firingin approached him in the late afternoon.

The old man hooted his pleasure at the outcome of a move in the game and did not look up. Firingin, reticent about what he had to tell Jeiso, did not interrupt.

Village women worked in the courtyard, returning scattered possessions to their dwellings. Hurried in their labor, the women rushed in and out of the low huts, moving armloads of clothing and cooking goods into darkened interiors. As they toiled, their voices rose, high pitched and excited, wailing mixed with staccato sounds of Rendille cross talk.

Firingin allowed his gaze to dwell on the smashed roofs of nearby dwellings. The sadness over what he had brought to the community rose in his throat and stuck like a heavy food.

Jeiso and his partner continued to play, oblivious to the chaos around them. Firingin grew impatient and considered returning to Leslie's hut. Darkness would soon come, and much preparation remained before he and his wife could leave.

Still, he must speak to his grandfather. The reasons for the going and the directions to the village of Firingin's real father, these would take much time to discuss, too much to be put off until the saying of goodbyes.

He waited, and moments later, a squeal of triumph ended the game.

Jeiso, smiling over his victory, turned his face to the towering figure of his grandson. "Please sit," he said, and started to arrange the beads for another contest.

Firingin thrust an arm forward.

"I must speak to you."

The old one stared a moment, then waved his game partner away.

His eyes glistened with fear. "What is it?"

Firingin looked toward the noisy women and the men standing near the game area.

"I would speak in a quiet place where no other can hear."

Brow wrinkled with concerned, Jeiso stared an instant then stood and pointed to a remote dwelling, the abode of one of his junior wives.

"If she is gone, we will talk by her place."

Firingin followed the patriarch to the entrance of the low structure and waited while Jeiso leaned down for a look inside.

"She is away, at her chores, I think," said Jeiso and motioned for Firingin to sit by the doorway.

Both men sat, and neither spoke. Only the distant, birdlike sounds of children bringing goats to the village could be heard.

Firingin stared at the ground. Though he must say his words to Jeiso, he had no desire for them. The leaving of the community where he had found his real family, the place where he had discovered freedom from the shame of being a Samburu herdsboy, and where he had felt the honor of becoming a leader among men, such would not be easy to tell.

He looked up and saw Jeiso waiting.

He started. "Before night comes..."

He saw Jeiso look longingly toward the place where others still played at bau. He must hurry and speak his message before the old man bolted.

He blurted out the main part. "Before this night's darkness comes, Grandfather, Leslie and I will leave your village."

Jeiso's mouth opened, and he rubbed a hand across his lips. "I do not understand. You and your woman have a good life here. For three round moons you have lived well among us. You have married and you have grown in stature." He paused, staring at Firingin. Then he added, "You must not let the dark devils chase you away."

Dark devils: Jeiso's words for the police flying machines that had invaded the community that afternoon. Firingin had seen the helicopters screaming in the sky when he'd returned from watering the camels, and he'd seen the giant birds leaving. He'd hurried to the courtyard, and he'd seen the destruction left by the soldiers. At Leslie's dwelling, he'd found his wife unhurt but crying tears of terror and despair. She'd told him that the Kenyans had come to take her away. "I told them no," she'd said, and she'd trembled as she'd added that the police would return and that the life she and Firingin had known was over. In that moment of sadness, Firingin had thought of escape. He'd told Leslie that they would go to the village of his real father, the man Jeiso had told him about, a Rendille elder thought to live in the north. It would be a place he'd said where she could have a new life, where she could start another school, and where their child could be born in safety.

Jeiso's voice interrupted, "I cannot sit here while you think thoughts. Tell me now why it is you speak of leaving us."

Firingin answered, "I speak of it because leaving here is what Leslie and I must do. The soldiers will return."

"No, they are gone now. They will not..."

Firingin held up a hand. "I must tell you all of this."

Jeiso rolled his eyes skyward.

"Grandfather, the soldiers will come. Leslie has told me they will, and she knows of such things. They will come back to your village, and when they do, they must not find Leslie here, and they..."

Again, Jeiso! "This day, the Kenyans tried to take your woman. One of them pushed her toward a flying machine with the point of his weapon... "

Firingin had not heard before of the pointing of a weapon. A flash of anger came but he said nothing.

"...I saw those things, but your Leslie was brave and told the Kenyan leader that she would not go. She wrote words on a paper. Words on paper have much power with the Kenyans. The leader of the soldiers looked upon those words, and he ordered his warriors to return to the machines. The dark devils then screamed with pain, rose from the earth and flew away. Why would those defeated ones come back again to our land?"

Firingin started to answer, but the old man wagged a finger to stop him.

A perplexed look showed in Jeiso's eyes, and he spoke with a questioning tone. "I saw today the power of your woman to chase the Kenyans away, yet I do not understand why they came for her. Perhaps, you can tell me this."

"That is part of what I need to talk to you about," said Firingin. "The Kenyans came to take Leslie because she was stolen."

A spark of revelation brightened Jeiso's eyes. "Stolen! So that is the answer. Through long hours of this afternoon, I have tried to think of the reason they had come for her, and now I know it."

He pointed at Firingin. "For your marriage, we did not pay the camels to the white elder who is Leslie's father."

Firingin raised a hand in protest, but Jeiso persisted. "You and I traded beasts, but I did not send any of those animals to the man who should have gotten them."

A cough shook the aged body, and Firingin watched with concern. His grandfather's health was not good.

Jeiso continued. "Here, in my village, you are already a man with status. Soon you will be the headman. This you know."

Firingin nodded. He knew of such plans, but he did not find pleasure in being reminded of the status he would soon leave behind.

"Wak will not wait long to call me," moaned Jeiso. "The women already talk of it in their daily circles. When I am gone, you will be the one who takes my place as village leader. You will hold all the wealth of the Hedaidile family, but you cannot keep that wealth if you owe camels."

Firingin smiled and shook his head. Jeiso often spoke of dying and of what will happen to the family treasure.

"Tomorrow," continued Jeiso, "I will tell Keigo to sort out eight beasts from my herd. And I will send a runner to South Horr with a message for the Kenyans. That message will tell them that you are now ready to make your payment to the white father."

Firingin pounded a fist on the ground. "No! Leslie's people do not want payment. She has already told me this."

Jeiso stared, startled by Firingin's outburst.

Quieter then, Firingin added, "The Kenyans came for Leslie, not because I did not pay. They came because she was taken from the tourist people by the Samburu."

Jeiso looked toward the horizon, his face twisted by confusion.

Firingin tendered the explanation. "The tourists stopped their movable dwelling on a road near Samburu villages, and Samburu people gathered around to see. A woman came from the tourist group and played with the village children. That woman was Leslie. While she played, a ball landed near a snake that hid under a bush. Leslie reached for the ball, and I threw my knife to kill the snake. Samburu warriors carried Leslie away from the road because they thought I had killed her with the knife."

Jeiso put his hands to his forehead. "The Samburu are crazy, but how could they think the woman was killed? She is alive. Even they must have seen that."

"When I threw my knife at the snake, the blade passed close to Leslie. She fell to the ground, and the warriors thought the weapon had hit her."

"Fools!" grumbled Jeiso. "The Samburu live as fools."

"It is true, those young ones were fools. They thought Leslie was dead, but she had only fainted. She fainted when she saw the snake. She has a great fear of looking on such animals."

Jeiso said nothing. He did not understand a fear of looking at snakes.

"When Leslie awakened from her fainting, the warriors became afraid. Some thought she had come back from the dead. They argued among themselves and then took her to the elders of their village. Leslie was kept in a dwelling while the elders talked of what to do, and within one day's time, Kenyan flying machines appeared in the skies, soldiers were seen on the roads and trails. The elders feared that the soldiers would come to the village and find the woman. They feared that dwellings would be destroyed and cattle would be run off."

Jeiso's eyes sparkled with interest.

Firingin continued. "The elders ordered Leslie returned to the tourist people, and they selected me to take her."

"You?"

"It was because of the Swahili language I speak. Those elders thought I could use my words to explain the warriors' mistake."

Jeiso shook his head.

"I took Leslie to the Kenyan town of Maralal, but before I could talk to the man I planned to return her to, a soldier came to the dwelling where I waited. I did not know the soldier and he could not have known me, but hate showed in that man's eyes. He pointed his rifle, searching toward the shadows where I hid."

The fearful memories brought a tightness to Firingin's throat. He stopped and took breath before continuing. "In the darkness, the soldier fired his weapon. He would have killed me with the flaming bullets, but I had moved behind him."

"And you killed the soldier."

Firingin nodded. "With the jeweled knife that you, my grandfather, now carry."

Jeiso's right hand drifted to his robes and touched the curved handle of his dagger.

"Honored Grandfather," said Firingin. "You must not keep that knife."

"But it is mine! Our trade was fair. I will not give it back."

Impressed by the intensity of Jeiso's protest, Firingin sat silent. He watched while his grandfather drew the magnificent weapon from under his wrap and held its blade skyward.

"Such a thing of beauty, I will never surrender," said Jeiso. "To do so, would dishonor Wak, Himself."

Against the afternoon sun, the rubies in the knife's handle glowed like coals of holy fire. Firingin waited in respectful silence until Jeiso lowered the dagger. Then, he spoke in a soft voice. "When I allowed you to trade for the knife, I did not believe the police would come to your village. But I was wrong. Today, they came, and they found Leslie here. As you have seen, she chased them away, but the tourist people want her back and the police will come again for her. She tells me this, and she has also told me that the police will come looking for me. They will look for me because of the stabbing of the soldier, and I am sure they will look for the knife I used."

Jeiso clutched the dagger as if to hide it against his body. "It is my knife. The Kenyans do not know that it killed the soldier."

"They do know. Look at the ring of rubies on the handle. Look and you will see that one is missing."

"I have seen that the jewel is missing. Nothing, even a dagger as beautiful as this, is perfect."

"That ruby was lost when I stabbed the soldier, and I believe the police have found it. They would have talked to the Samburu after they found it, and the Samburu would have told them that a knife with such rubies belonged to me."

A deep sadness moved across Jeiso's face.

"I will not take the knife from you, Grandfather. It is yours, and I can see that you must keep it. But the police must not find it in your village."

"The Kenyans are fools," whispered Jeiso. "I will hide the weapon where they will never find it."

Firingin smiled. "Yes, you must hide it. But not inside a dwelling or anywhere in the village.

You must hide the knife in the desert, in a place where the police could never know it is yours. Cover it with rocks and sand. Tonight you must do it, before tomorrow's sun rises."

Terror fixed a stare in Jeiso's eyes. "You think the soldiers will come tomorrow?"

"If not tomorrow, a day soon. Leslie has told me that their flying machines can take them to the great city in the south and back to this place in less than one passing of the sun."

He saw Jeiso's face hardened into a mask of fear. He needed to say words of encouragement. "If Leslie and I are not here, Grandfather, and the police do not find the knife, they will not stay in your village. As today, they will go when they find nothing. And they will not come back another time. They will look in the desert for Leslie and me, maybe in the villages near Samburu country. Hide the jeweled knife with great care, and the police will have no reason to harm you or the people of your village."

Jeiso's expression softened, and he turned the dagger slowly in his hands. "The Kenyans shall not find this knife. Not tomorrow or any day after tomorrow."

For a time, Firingin and Jeiso sat in silence. Then, Jeiso struggled as if to rise to his feet.

Firingin motioned for him to stay. "I have more I need to say."

Looking nervous, Jeiso forced a smile.

Firingin proceeded. "Tonight, Leslie and I will travel to the north. We wish to go to the village of the Rendille man you spoke of as my father."

Jeiso shook his head. "You will not find that man in any village north of here."

Firingin sat, stunned by the revelation.

Jeiso continued. "That community's well went dry, maybe two round moons ago. The people have all gone to Korr, a city with bountiful wells that lies far to the south and east."

"Korr?"

"Yes, it is one of the places you might have stopped when you were with Hedad."

Firingin nodded. He had, indeed, been near Korr with his now dead cousin's caravan. It was a town with a large number of Kenyan police. Hedad had warned him of them, and Firingin had waited outside in the desert.

Firingin looked toward the distant hills. He knew that he and Leslie would not go to Korr. A new plan was needed. His mind raced, thinking of other places. He had heard of Mount Kulal, a peak with rich grazing on its slopes. Perhaps he and Leslie could live in seclusion in one of its high valleys. Perhaps, but Leslie would be lonely in such a place. She wanted other women around, and she wanted her school. Places for building a new life might be found on the other side of the Chalbi Desert. He had heard of the country called Ethiopia, a land, it was said, not a part of Kenya. But so much desert would be difficult to cross. Perhaps too difficult for a woman who carried a child.

Jeiso sat watching.

Firingin spoke reassurance. "No matter. Leslie and I do not need to go to my father."

Jeiso grinned. "No, you can stay with us. We will hide you and your woman from the Kenyans."

Firingin shook his head. "Leslie and I cannot live hidden. We will travel far from here to a place where we can be safe. Maybe..."

He stopped. It would be better not to tell Jeiso where they might go.

"After a time, the Kenyans will forget about Leslie and me. We will wait in a distant place through one wet season, and then we will come back to you."

Jeiso's eyes squinted, showing doubt. In an attempt to convey confidence, Firingin spoke directions, using a strong voice. "When the police come to your village, you must tell them that you do not know where we are. Say to them that we left in secret, in the middle of the night. You may even tell them that you would have tried to stop us from going. Indeed, you have talked against it. Do those things and all will be well."

Jeiso's body shook with another wheezing cough. Looking desperate and weak, he whispered, "I will tell them those things, but this I know. Wak will not grant me many days and nights from this day. If you do not return before another wet season has passed, you will not find me here."

Firingin offered no comment.

Jeiso stood as if to end the conversation.

Firingin rose to his feet and stood beside him.

Jeiso spoke. "You will take the young she-camel I gave you?" The question showed that Jeiso no longer fought the leaving.

Firingin nodded. "I will take her."

"But your woman cannot ride that wild one."

"Leslie will ride on my shoulders. She traveled thus when we came from the South."

"But she is with child. She must not sit with her legs astride your neck."

Feeling anger and wanting to end the talking before regrettable words were said, Firingin took a step away from his grandfather.

Jeiso put out a hand. He spoke with a low voice. "I have more to say."

Firingin waited.

"The old she-camel from Hedad's caravan, she is a beast with an easy ride. Your Leslie has already found her so."

Firingin nodded. He remembered the trip from Ilaut made with Leslie and the man who had once been his best friend. Firingin closed his eyes and again saw the image of his cousin's death, the hand reaching from the sand.

Jeiso's talk continued. "If you will not stay with us, my grandson, you must travel well from here. The old she-camel will make the ride better for your woman. I will lend that beast to you, and you can bring her back when you return."

"Your generosity is great, Grandfather."

Jeiso produced a tight-lipped smile and nodded his head in the direction of Leslie's dwelling. "Go now. Go to your woman before the water of my eyes betrays me."

"Later, I will bring Leslie to see you. She will want to say goodbye."

Jeiso nodded.

The golden glow of a desert sunset had colored the skies by the time Leslie returned to the empty structure of her former home. Throughout the late afternoon, she had visited dwellings in the village, said farewell to her many friends and given away things too heavy to carry on the trip.

Firingin sat by the hut's doorway. He had taken all of the packages to the corral and now waited to tell Leslie of the change in their plans. He had decided that the direction of their travel would still be north, but how far they would now travel, he did not know.

He could see the emotion showing on his wife's face as she sat down beside him. She spoke with a sad voice about the children from her school, how they had stood, wide-eyed and silent in the dwellings of their mothers. Some of the braver students had pleaded for Leslie to stay. She told Firingin of needing to clamp her teeth over the quivering of her lips.

"I feel so guilty," she wailed.

"Guilty" was not one of the words of English he had learned from her, but he would not interrupt for an explanation.

"Those children need me here. They need me, and what do I

do? Go running off like a scared rabbit." More words he did not know, but he felt the meaning. He asked, "You have... how do you say it? Two thoughts?"

That brought a smile, and always the teacher, she corrected him. "Second thoughts. That's what you mean. In other words, changed my mind."

He nodded.

"No, I haven't changed my mind. I know that the police will be back here soon—as soon as they get my deportation papers."

Deportation? Another English word. Confused, he asked her to clarify. "Your words—I do not understand them. Do you wish to wait here for de-poor-tashun papers?"

"No, we have to leave. We can't even consider staying—not even another day."

She looked hard into his eyes. "Firingin, I want to be with you. More than anything, I want us to have our life together. I want to have our baby in this country, and I want live among the Rendille people and teach school for their children."

Not knowing if they would find a place of safety in Rendille country, he made no comment.

Leslie kept on talking. "You have no idea what it's like to have students who really want to learn like the ones in this village."

It was true, he knew nothing of such things.

"Besides," she continued, "I have no reason to go back to America. I have no close friends or family there--not since Aunt Jean died."

He nodded. He had heard before about Leslie's aunt who died.

Without warning, Leslie jumped to her feet and ran. Firingin stood and would have tried to stop her, but she ran only a short distance and stopped herself at the entrance of a nearby dwelling, the abode of the woman named Wambila, her best friend. Even at the time for the evening meal, Wambila motioned for Leslie to enter. Leslie crawled into the doorway, and soon, the muffled sounds of two women crying came from inside the structure.

The sun had set, and the sky had darkened when Leslie returned from Wambila's dwelling. She came to Firingin, still sobbing, and he held her body with his arms. He knew she would be comforted by such holding. He would wait for another time to tell her about the changing of plans.

They stood together, and when she stopped crying, she spoke in a brave sounding voice. "I'm ready to go now."

They ate a cold meal, food saved back from the packing, and they went to say their goodbyes to Jeiso.

L eslie stood at the edge of the village corral and watched
while Firingin sorted bundles for the load. Her body shud-
dered, and without thinking, she closed her eyes. For what must
have been the thousandth time, she saw images of the police heli-
copters.

How could she have known they would have come so far for
her? Of course, she might have guessed. She was, after all, a tourist
who'd been taken from her group right in the middle of a Kenyan
road. And as far as the police had known, until today, she'd been
held against her will by a man they sought for murder. A murderer,
that's what they thought Firingin was. Never mind he'd been trying
to return her when the Kenyan military had come at him with guns
blazing.

After Firingin had returned from the trading expedition he'd
been on with his cousin Hedad, he'd told her that officers were
searching as far north as the desert community of Korr. Concerned
about the danger presented to his grandfather's village, Firingin had
said that he and Leslie must return to Maralal. It was then she'd
told him that she was pregnant with his child.

He hadn't known before, and after getting over the initial shock,
he'd said that such a thing could not be. Unwed, tribal women are

not allowed to give birth. When the pregnancies are discovered, they are always aborted. Firingin had known that custom and so had Leslie. She'd been told by Wambila when she'd gone to her friend after the morning sickness had become too persistent to be ignored.

Horrified by the cruel practice, Leslie had quickly formulated a way around it. With Wambila's help, she'd keep the pregnancy a secret until Firingin returned. Then she'd give him the news, and he would agree to a quick wedding.

At the time, she and Firingin had been together about two and a half months—without a calendar it's difficult to be exact. They had lived together and survived together in all kinds of situations, and they'd loved each other intensely. She wouldn't have considered an early marriage if the circumstances hadn't demanded it, but what else could she have done? The life of her child—his child—had hung in the balance. Marriage was only way to save it. Returning to Maralal, as Firingin had said, would have been impossible. A trip of a hundred miles or more would have been too long for a woman carrying a child.

Firingin had been one the most caring people she'd ever known—certainly the most caring man. She'd expected him to go along with the idea of getting married as soon as she proposed it, but she'd been wrong. Firingin had answered that he could not marry, that among the Samburu, only adult men were allowed to take wives, and because of a tribal ruling, he was not an adult and never would be.

Hurt and angered by his crazy excuse, she'd screamed and cried in frustration. He'd reacted to the outburst by showing the same tenderness he'd presented so often to her, and eventually she'd calmed herself. They'd then considered options. He'd offered to speak to his grandfather about Rendille rules for marriage.

Jeiso had immediately given their wedding his blessing. He'd said that Firingin could not be bound by Samburu constraints, that his mother, Jeiso's eldest daughter, had carried him, her first-born, when she'd left to marry her Samburu husband. The real father was a Rendille elder from a nearby village, the man, Leslie believed, she and Firingin would soon be meeting for the first time.

She touched her abdomen, and she smiled at the thought of her child being born in the new village. She imagined the joy of having her baby in her arms, also the pleasure of meeting new friends and the thrill of starting another school. It wouldn't be the same. That she realized. But, hopefully, it would be a place where the police and their menacing helicopters would never come.

Walking slowly around the two camels of his caravan, Firingin made what appeared to be the last inspection before departure. The heifer camel pulled at its rope. He stopped and checked the knot. Satisfied, he stepped back and gazed a moment at the grumpy-looking creature. Then he turned his eyes to Leslie and motioned for her. It was time to go.

She cringed at the thought of actually leaving. Still, the trip would be short, two days, maybe only one. Even that amount of travel had concerned her at first. Early in the afternoon, she'd gone to Wambila to seek advice on how a pregnant woman might make such a journey. Wambila, in addition to being Leslie's best friend, had been the woman assigned, after the wedding, to be her midwife.

Regal looking, as usual, Wambila had been working inside her dwelling when Leslie stooped to the doorway. She motioned for Leslie to enter and indicated a stack of blankets for sitting.

"What a catastrophy!" said Wambila in her near-perfect English. "Did they do this much damage at your place?"

"They took some of my school notes, nothing more." Wambila looked puzzled. "School notes? How strange. Why would they only take bits of paper from you and throw everything in the courtyard for the rest of us?"

Not wanting to get involved in a discussion of what the police had done, Leslie said nothing. She pondered how she might work in her first question about the trip.

Without warning, Wambila's youngest son, Jesu, rushed into the dwelling. "Teacher, teacher," he shouted, "why are you going away from here? Don't you like us anymore?"

Astounded that plans, less than an hour old, had become public knowledge, Leslie didn't respond.

Wambila grabbed the child and forced him to sit. "Pay attention to your manners, young man. If you want to ask teacher a question, speak with respect. Then, perhaps, she will answer."

The boy repeated his concerns with more polite phrasing, and both he and his mother stared, waiting for Leslie to speak.

Leslie searched her mind for the right words. She didn't want to tell anybody, certainly not Wambila, that Firingin was running from the police.

"It will be a short trip," she offered. "Just to a nearby village. Firingin's father..."

The boy jumped to his feet and raced outside, yelling loud enough to be heard all the way to the corral. "She is going! Our teacher is leaving us."

Wambila looked hurt.

"We won't be gone forever," said Leslie. "Firingin and I will be coming back... Soon, I hope."

Wambila covered her open mouth. She stared at Leslie. "It's the police, isn't it? They came here about you, didn't they? That's why they only took your school notes."

Leslie sat looking at Wambila, the friend with whom she shared everything, even the forbidden pregnancy. How could she even consider deceiving such a person?

She decided that she had to reveal part of the problem with the Kenyans. Nodding, she answered, "You're right. They wanted to take me to Niarobi with them... to make me return to America."

Wambila gave a thoughtful stir to the pot of porridge on the back of her hearth.

"But they left without you."

Leslie volunteered her explanation. "I told them I wouldn't go, that I'd complain to the U.S. Embassy if they forced me."

"Embussee? It is a word I do not know."

Leslie tendered a short answer. "It is a place of great power."

Wambila's eyes widened. "Power enough to scare away the Kenyan Police?" To Wambila, or anyone else in the village, it would be inconceivable that any thing or any body could frighten the Kenyan Police.

Leslie nodded to the question.

Wambila smiled a wary smile. "All right, I guess I'll accept that. Anyway, the police are gone and you're still here.... But why then are you leaving?"

Leslie let out a long breath and looked toward the ceiling. "Like I said before. To stay for a short time with Firingin's father." The hurt look returned to Wambila's eyes. She turned from Leslie and started to move boxes of clothing against the back wall.

Leslie reached and touched her shoulder. "Please don't be angry."

Wambila jerked away and said nothing. After a time she spoke, using a clinical sounding tone. "You will need a midwife in your new village."

Leslie smiled. "That's what I came to talk about. Going on the trip."

Wambila did not return the smile. "I don't suppose you'll tell me where the village is."

"I can't. I don't even know myself. Firingin..."

"Men!" hissed Wambila. "They tell us nothing."

"I don't think Firingin knows. I think he's talking to Jeiso, maybe right now, to find out where to go."

Wambila ignored the explanation. "A trip to a nearby settlement should be no problem. You must take normal precautions. Eat good food."

"I'll certainly try to do that."

"Don't forget your fever pills."

Leslie nodded. Wambila's reference to the malaria tablets showed that the story about a short stay hadn't been believed.

"Most communities aren't as prosperous as this one," added Wambila. "You may not find all the things you need. You should take plenty of millet with you, and several boxes of dates."

"I'll pack a week's supply."

"At least that much. And Firingin—he should take a goat for milk."

"I don't think he's taking any animals other than his young heifer." She hadn't known at the time that Jeiso would be lending the old camel. Wambila continued. "I'll give you a bottle of cow's blood. No milk in it. Milk would make it spoil. Get that man of yours to draw blood from his beast. You must drink it fresh, so he should draw some every other day."

Leslie nodded. There had been a time when she'd rebelled against drinking blood, but no longer. Concern for the health and strength of her baby had forced her to overcome such squeamishness.

"And whenever you can, buy fresh fruit and vegetables. Also fish and meat."

"We may not see any markets."

Wambila smiled a patient smile. "Whenever you can. Eventually, food traders come to all the villages. If you'd have stayed here, you'd have seen one."

Ignoring the dig, Leslie asked about the effects of walking long distances.

"It should not be a problem Though you're not as strong as most women. But, in the fourth month, I wouldn't worry—even if the trek is a week or longer—once you've gained some strength in your legs."

Saddened by the growing hostility in Wambila's voice, Leslie abandoned the rest of her questions. She tried to think of words she might say to ease the hurt feelings, but Wambila returned to stacking boxes, and Leslie realized the conversation had ended. Feeling a deep despair over what had happened, she left and returned to her own dwelling.

Later, she'd impulsively gone back to her friend, and the two women had hugged and cried like lost children.

Firingin held out a hand. "I must now lift you up."

She hesitated. "I don't need to ride. My feet are fine, and

Wambila says I must build strength in my legs."

Firingin looked at her, his eyes showed the thinness of his patience. "The camels walk fast," he said and then hefted her to the blanket-padded seat inside the load-carrier's frame.

Remembering their last caravan together, she smiled down at him. "Just like old times."

He didn't smile back. Without a word, he walked to the front of the column and emitted a low whistle. The camels' ears flicked forward, and the creatures moved, with a shambling gait, toward the far end of the corral.

High above, Leslie looked out on the darkened village. Only Jeiso's main lodge and a few others showed the glow of oil lamps. She looked for the empty structure where she and Firingin had lived and loved, but could not pick it out. She felt her eyes moisten. She rubbed savagely with the backs of her hands.

The column stopped in front of the corral gate. There would be a short wait while a village elder, a man named Keigo, moved the barrier aside.

Several animals of the resident herd rested near the exit, lumpy-looking in the darkness. One raised its head and sniffed as if to show disdain for the departing procession. The animal's theatrics brought a weak smile to Leslie.

Firingin bade farewell to Keigo, and the caravan moved into the open desert.

Soon the train of two camels climbed laboriously up a pathway toward the nearby hills. Firingin did not look back. He seemed angry, but Leslie knew it was sadness that kept his eyes away. At the high point of the trail, she tried to see down to the village. Ridge tops crowded the foreground and blocked her view.

The caravan pitched onto a long, descending incline, and the old camel braked with jolting, load-tossing steps until the route reached the level plain of a wide and featureless wadi.

Firingin picked up his pace, and the camel's motion became less rough but more rhythmic and monotonous. In time Leslie dropped into a shallow sleep. She dreamed. Not a pleasant dream, but one that took her back to Cleveland and her seventh-grade class-room. Images of the Kenyan police mingled with those of cater-wauling teenagers, and Leslie perceived herself trying to get away.

A grittiness invaded the dream, then came a sound of moaning. Leslie awoke, and disoriented she blinked into a moonless dark-ness. Through curtains of blowing sand, she saw the figure of Firingin, walking, bowed into the gale.

She shouted out, "Shouldn't we stop?"

He seemed not to hear.

She waited for a break in the gusts, then yelled again.

He pulled the caravan to a halt and walked back to her. "Are you all right?" He seemed not to notice the onslaught of raging air.

She answered that she was okay and then asked if he didn't think they should find shelter.

He looked at the sky and toward the distant hills and actually said that it was a small wind. She would have told him that it wasn't at all small to her, but the young camel came barging to the front and stood between them.

With characteristic patience, Firingin led the animal to the rear, and when he returned, he informed Leslie that they would be stop-ping in the morning, at an oasis.

"An oasis in the morning? I don't understand."

He seemed to ignore her question, and she asked again, "If this storm won't stop us, why don't we just keep going until we reach the village?"

"It might be a long trip," he answered.

A blast of sand forced her to duck behind the collar of her wrap. What does he mean by a long trip? When a lull came, she raised her head. She would have asked Firingin to repeat his words, but he had gone to his post and had started pulling the caravan forward.

Soon the camel resumed its ship of the desert motion. Leslie curled her body against the blowing and tried not to think about a longer trip.

Perhaps, she hadn't heard right. The blasting of the wind could have easily distorted the sound. She'd ask again in the morning .

3

When Leslie first shouted, Firingin had been deep in thought about the trip ahead.

After one day's travel, his small caravan would leave the lands near Jeiso's village. Only instinct and, at night, the star on the horizon would then guide him. He would have to use everything he knew about the northern country just to keep Leslie, the camels and himself alive.

He would not go westward. The high places there might bring coolness and perhaps water, but the climbing and the descending would bring discomfort to Leslie and would tire the camels. Beyond the western mountains stretched the great sea called Turkana. The fierce warriors who lived near that sea were known to attack caravans. Goods were said to be taken and people were killed. With limbs, sometimes heads, severed, bodies had been found lying in pools of their own blood, abandoned among piles of debris. He would not take his caravan near the land of the Turkana. To the east the Chalbi Desert loomed as a heated furnace over a waterless plain.

Tales had been told of dry rivers in the Chalbi, streams that flowed with sand instead of moisture, and sink holes that could swallow camels and drivers deep into the earth. He must take care to stay away from such hazards.

Rendille and also the Gabbra lived in many regions of the north. The Rendille would offer friendship, but the Gabbra would be enemies. The Rendille and the Gabbra had fought for many seasons over places to graze their animals. Gabbra warriors would not welcome a lone Rendille traveler to their lands. He would avoid the Gabbra but also those of his own tribe. He had already brought too much trouble to his family's people.

A watering hole would be reached at morning's light. It would be a place with trees where Leslie could rest. For a few hours, she could stretch in the shade, but the sun would soon bring its burning heat and would end her comfort. Then, they would go again—northward. He knew of no other watering holes in the lands they would cross. Many days might pass before Leslie could lie again in a place with shade.

He thought of food and water. Somehow he must find what they needed. Hedad had taught him only a little about tubers and plants.

The second shout from Leslie interrupted his thoughts. He looked and saw her leaning forward on the camel's back.

He held the rope, and the old beast shuffled to a halt. He walked to Leslie and asked if she was all right. She answered that she was, but she complained, about the wind.

He looked toward the zenith. Stars showed through the clouds. He thought for a moment.

He hated to see Leslie frightened, but the blowing would not get worse. Soon it would be over.

"It is only a small wind," he answered. "Before we could make our camp it would be gone from here."

She had started to say something more, but the heifer camel interfered by coming to the front of the caravan. He prodded the impetuous creature back to its place, and when he returned to Leslie, he tried to make a joke. "That one would become our leader if I let her."

Leslie seemed not to hear, and he thought it better not to repeat his poor attempt. In a louder voice, he told her that they would stop at the oasis.

She shouted back, asking why they needed an oasis.

He did not understand her objection.

She spoke of going on to his father's village. He must tell her that the plans had changed.

He said that it might be a long trip.

She made no reply but covered her head against a strong gust. He returned to his post. He tugged the column forward, and he wondered if he might not have said more than was wise. His words about the long trip could bring worry to Leslie.

So newly a man, there was much he needed to learn of the way a husband must talk to a wife.

A painful cramp developed in Leslie's right leg. She tried rubbing it, but the pain only got worse.

For the third time in less than an hour, she shouted to Firingin. He promptly pulled the column to a halt, and looking alarmed, hurried back.

"Is something wrong?"

She reached down for him. "Help me off. I need to walk a little."

He lifted her from the camel, and she took a few steps holding onto his shoulder.

The stiffness eased a bit. She hobbled away from the caravan, going several yards in front and then back. More improvement. She told Firingin that she wanted to stop riding for a while. "If I walk, it might keep the muscles from tightening." She gestured to show what she meant by "tightening."

He stared. "You think your feet are ready for this walking?"

She understood his concern. Soreness in her feet had been a major problem on the trek from Maralal.

"My feet are okay. It's my leg that's hurting, and I need to loosen it up a little."

Firingin took her left hand in his, placed it on the adult camel's lead rope and forced the fingers into a tight grip. "You must not let this be loose. If you do, you can become lost in the blowing sand."

As if to emphasize his point, a hard gust blasted a cloud of grit-laden air over them.

Leslie held onto the rope, and after the wind subsided, Firingin added, "You must cry out if you cannot keep up."

She nodded, and he whistled the caravan forward.

The fast start forced Leslie to run a few steps, but determined not to call another halt, she lengthened her stride and kept pace at Firingin's shoulder.

He smiled at her. "Soon the land will cool. When it is no longer too warm for the air, the winds will stop."

She nodded, and they both leaned into a another cell of the agitated atmosphere.

Before morning light, Leslie was back on the camel. Firingin had noticed her lagging, and without asking, he'd lifted her to the carrier. As predicted, the blowing had stopped. With the stillness, the sky had cleared to produce a spectacular, after-midnight show of stars. Leslie gazed upward, craning her neck to see the Milky Way. She loved looking at the night sky over the desert. In Jeiso's village she'd often enjoyed the celestial show, but she'd never seen it so bright and beautiful as this.

In time, the rocking of the camel and Leslie's exhaustion collaborated to lull her back into sleep. She dreamed again, but a dream less disturbing than before. On her undulating perch she rode in fitful slumber until the buffeting of morning breezes stirred her to consciousness.

Numb and groggy, she sat, reluctant to move for fear of bringing forth some deep and dormant pain.

Firingin seemed to be walking even faster. She wondered why. To her query, he answered, "The camels smell water. It would take much work to hold them back."

Makes sense, she thought, but scanning the surrounding terrain, she saw nothing that would indicate water, only barren ridges, rising and falling to the right and to the left. The land supported little vegetation other than thorn bushes. Wiry and armed with their arsenals of spikes, those plants invaded the many fissures in the fields of millions, perhaps zillions, of rocks and pebbles.

A line of the shrubs climbed the side of a nearby hill, sentinels against an unseen enemy in a kingdom of desolation. Seeking relief from the harsh scenery at ground level, she shifted her gaze to the sky.

Pale, almost white, the canopy glared back at her. The crystal view of early morning had succumbed to an eruption of wind-borne particles.

"How far to the water?" she asked Firingin's back.

His head turned a degree or two. "Not far."

Shuffling and rocking, the charge toward unseen moisture continued until, without warning, the caravan turned and came to a shuddering stop.

Leslie looked back at the former pathway, and she saw a ten-foot snake moving swiftly toward a depression in the field of wind-swept pebbles. When the creature stopped, it was no more than twenty feet from the fidgeting pair of camels.

"Do not show your eyes," whispered Firingin.

Leslie obeyed, quickly pulling her wrap over her face. She hated snakes more than any other thing in the desert.

Again Firingin's voice. "Another one."

Through the folds of her robe, she saw the second snake, an animal almost as large as the first. It slithered past the place where Firingin stood and came to rest alongside its companion.

"Spitting cobras," said Firingin, "a male and a wife out hunting for their morning meal."

Spitting cobras! Leslie knew about those awful things. But husband and wife? How can he possibly think of snakes that way?

Looking from behind a sleeve, she saw Firingin turn his eyes skyward and recite a string of words. She couldn't make out what he'd said, but as soon as he finished, he looked at her and said that the cobras were gone.

A cautious scan toward the depression revealed that the ser-

pents had, indeed, vanished. Magic? Probably just a timely depar-
ture into an underground lair. Whatever it was, she'd take it.

A whistle from Firingin, and the camels resumed their trot to-
ward water.

Alert for more of the reptile family, Leslie rode in silence. She
saw no brothers or sisters, or any other crawling relatives, but after
perhaps ten minutes of looking ahead, she noticed what had to be a
spot of darkness on the shimmering horizon.

"Is that our famous oasis?" she asked, pointing.

Firingin grinned back at her. "Our oasis, yes. Once again the
star of the north has proved faithful."

Another ten minutes, or so, and the spot had resolved itself into
a pitiful looking stand of wind ravaged palm trees.

Firingin steered his beasts toward an open place in the middle
of the grove.

A pair of jackals ran wildly from a nearby clump of bushes, and
Firingin forced the column to jerky stop.

"Scavengers," he announced, "A caravan must have been here
in the night."

He looked intently at the hilltops, first those behind then the
ones ahead. Suddenly, without saying a word, he urged his animals
away from the path to the oasis and toward the closest hills at the
side of the now narrow valley.

Leslie scanned the ridges, and in the distance, beyond the oasis,
she saw three men standing.

Each held a rifle in his hands!

"Who...?"

Firingin's gesture stopped her in mid-question. He led the col-
umn into a small canyon, and behind a low embankment, pulled
the camels to a halt. He motioned for Leslie to dismount. She
extended her arms, and with one quick move he lowered her to the
ground.

She stood, staring at him, her heart pounding a drumbeat of
fear.

Firingin pointed in the direction of the three men.

"I saw," she whispered.

He nodded. Then he commanded the old camel to kneel. When the beast had levered herself down, he placed the end of the lead rope in Leslie's hands.

"Hold her," he said in a low voice. "Keep her calm. Stroke the side of her face."

Leslie crouched beside the camel's head, and Firingin brought the heifer forward and tied it close to the lead animal's nose. He petted the heifer a few times and made a clucking sound. The heifer laid down.

He looked again in the direction of the men but said nothing. Giving a palms-down signal for Leslie to stay, he assumed a bent-over stance and moved quickly to the base of the embankment. He worked his way along the base toward the mouth of canyon.

The heifer flailed its legs as if to get up, and Leslie, fearing that the creature might escape or bawl out, tried to make clucking sounds. The older camel seemed to understand that silence was required. She lay still as a rock, and the heifer, tied eyeball to eyeball with the elder beast, succumbed to the glare of superior authority.

With her charges settled, Leslie turned her attention back to Firingin. He had ended his crouching walk at a large thorn bush, and there he knelt, looking through a tangle toward the ridge where the men must have still been standing.

After several minutes of staring, Firingin hunkered his way back into the canyon. When he reached Leslie, he leaned down and said one raspy word:

Turkana!

5

The approach of the first snake, on a path straight toward the caravan, brought pleasure to Firingin. In Samburu traditions of his former life, serpents come to greet twin children born to a family. Twins and snakes are thought to be natural friends since snakes are believed to be born in pairs. If the serpent's coming meant that Leslie would bear twin babies, she should have no further need for her fearing of the animals.

He saw that the snake was a cobra of the spitting kind, and he feared that he might be wrong about it bringing good fortune. He halted the camels, and cautioned Leslie to cover her eyes.

The second snake could have been the twin of the first or perhaps its mate. He told Leslie that it was the mate and muttered a prayer, asking Nkai, the Samburu God, to remove the creatures.

The serpents disappeared into a crack in the ground, and Firingin mouthed thanks to the God.

He told Leslie that the snakes were gone, and restarted the caravan in the direction of the oasis.

Leslie said nothing. He knew her fear of snakes was strong, and he wondered if that fear might have taken her voice away.

After a time, she asked about the oasis. Pleased to hear her speaking, he answered in a playful way, telling her about the guide star.

They continued northward, and not far from the watering place, two jackals ran from a bush near the pathway and fled to the nearby hills. Scavengers, the creatures might have been foraging where a recent caravan had camped.

He stopped his column and scanned the valley, also the ridges. He saw nothing until he focused his eyes on the bluff that over-looked the oasis from the other side. There, he saw three men stand-ing. Each held a shooting weapon.

Taking advantage of the early warning given by the jackals, Firingin pulled his camels toward a small ravine at the side of the valley. Though the men with the rifles appeared to be unaware of Firingin's caravan, it would be wise to seek a place of concealment. Leslie started to ask a question. He stopped her.

Within minutes they were inside the canyon, but its walls were not high. The lead camel's back and Leslie, on top, were not hid-den. He halted the column and had Leslie dismount. He then kneeled the beast behind the ridge.

He asked if Leslie had seen the men. She had.

He handed her the lead rope and brought the heifer forward. He calmed the young creature, and tied her nose to nose with the she-camel.

After watching to be sure the camels were quiet, he told Leslie to stay with them. Then he walked, crouching low, toward a large thorn bush at the mouth of the ravine. From a place behind the tangle of branches, he looked out at the men. They seemed preoc-cupied with watching to the west; they had not seen Firingin's cara-van approach from the south.

He observed scarring on the men's arms. He squinted to sharpen his vision and saw the marks to be great in number. The men were Turkana warriors, hard-eyed veterans of many murderous campaigns. One of the warriors carried scarring on both his right and left arms. That man had taken the lives of women and children along with those of men.

Firingin crawled back to Leslie and told her that the ones on the bluff were Turkana. He told her that she must be prepared to hide if the warriors came toward them.

"I will go and watch, but you must watch me. If I raise my hand as a signal, leave the beasts and run to the bushes high in the ravine." He pointed to show her the place where the bushes grew. "There you must hide until it is safe."

She asked how she would know when it was safe.

For that, he had no answer.

Back at the thorn bush, he noted that the Turkana were ill prepared for the killing they practiced. Empty loops in the belts across their bodies showed that they had few bullets left for their weapons. The state of their clothing and their physical condition showed a weakness in them for any kind of fighting.

He saw the Turkana gesture. Perhaps they argued. The distance was too great for their words to come to him. One, maybe the leader, motioned toward a place behind some rocks.

More Turkana came forth, five women and several children. Two of the women and an older boy led a column of seven heavily loaded donkeys. The man who seemed to be the leader pointed to the west, and soon the entire group moved off the bluff and into the wadi.

Firingin watched the Turkana go. He watched until they and their donkeys climbed into the high hills on the opposite side of the valley. He waited a time. The sun climbed in the sky, and no Turkana returned. He went back to Leslie.

"They have gone. Those raiders have been many days on their trip of plunder, and they now go back to their home villages."

"Their home villages? How do you know that? Maybe they've only gone for firewood?"

He shook his head. "The men went. Even among Turkana, men do not gather firewood. The donkeys are loaded with great quantities of goods the Turkana have stolen. Those bandits now return with the plunder to their homes by the lake."

"But, there might be more around, don't you think?"

"I think there are no more here. The Turkana do not share

what they steal. If others were near, these would not have traveled so boldly in the open."

He untied the heifer and made the camels stand. After lifting Leslie to her seat, he steered the column toward the head of the ravine then along the ridges above the grove of trees. Neither men nor other camels were seen, and Firingin guided his beasts into the valley. Minutes later, the procession shuffled to a halt under the ragged stem of a dead palm.

He took a wary look around, then helped Leslie off the she-camel. Leslie walked a few steps. He started unloading cooking pots and food. Leslie took the millet and the grinding tools to a place in the shade where she would sit and mash grain for the morning porridge. She had learned, in the village, the wifely duty of grinding millet for the meals. Firingin brought sticks and built a small fire. He noticed that Leslie remained silent. Her gaze shifted, searching the surrounding hills. He told her not to worry. She smiled a weak smile, and he left her with her work. He led the camels to the spring for a drink. Though they had hurried toward the smell of water, the beasts drank little and splashed at the liquid with their muzzles.

Firingin hobbled the she-camel in the shade of one of the palms and tied the heifer to a strong trunk.

When he returned to the campsite, he saw that Leslie had not finished the millet. She was often slow with her grinding.

He poured water for their tea. She looked away from him, and he wondered if she might be bothered by more than fear of the Turkana. He asked if she wanted to sleep before eating. She shook her head.

With an accusing voice, she asked if she had heard him right in the night.

He knew nothing of what she had heard in the night.

She asked if he had said something about the trip to his father's village lasting longer than a day or two.

He answered, "I have said nothing in the night about my father's village."

"But, I heard you say words that sounded like our trip would be longer. It was when we stopped the first time in the storm."

She still thought the evening winds were a storm.

"Well, was I hallucinating or what?"

He did not know the strange word she used, but he remembered that he'd tried to tell her at their first stop that the trip would be longer. He also remembered his regret of saying that thing, and his worry that the words might have brought distress.

He studied Leslie's face to see if anger showed.

It did not.

He asked if she wished to talk before eating about the way they would go on the trip.

She nodded. "I think I should, at least, find out if there has been a change."

He tried to think of how he would tell about the uncertainty that had come to their travel. After seeing the Turkana, even the plans he'd made to travel north near the mountains were no longer good. From here, he must take a different route, one where chances of encountering more of the Turkana would be small.

He would not turn around and go south. There were no places of safety for his wife and child in the south.

"Well," said Leslie, the word stretching out. "How far is it to your father's village?"

"It does not matter how far it is to that place. We are not going there. The village is gone."

"Gone?" What are you talking about? That's the place Jeiso..."

Firingin had raised a hand. "Jeiso has told me different. Yesterday, he said the people of my father's village have all gone to live in Korr."

"Korr? That's somewhere south of here, isn't it? We're not going south, are we?"

Firingin shook his head. "I will not go to Korr. The police are there."

At an earlier time, he had thought of surrendering himself to the police at Korr. He had thought that once, but now he had responsibilities: a wife, and soon a child to care for. He...

"But where then are we going?"

He tried to speak an answer. "I have thought of going to a far place, a land called Ethiopia. Hedad spoke of it..."

"Ethiopia!" Her voice came as a scream. "Ethiopia must be over a hundred miles from here!"

He knew not the distance she spoke of.

Leslie's voice softened. "Why don't we just stop at the next Rendille village we come to? They'll be happy to take us in. They all know your grandfather, don't they?"

Those words brought anger to Firingin. *She does not know the customs of the Rendille people. She cannot say what they will do.*

He tried to keep calm when he spoke. "I will not bring police danger to the villages of Rendille I do not know."

Her eyes flashed. "But you would have brought danger to the village of your father. He's Rendille isn't he?"

More anger: *She does not even understand that a father must give help to a son. How can I talk to her of this?*

He spoke to end her questions. "We must go to a place where the police will not come. I will think later of where it will be."

"And I'm supposed to just follow along blindly...to God knows..."

He held up a hand. "You have said that you would not stay and wait for the soldiers to come. You have said this, and now you tell me that I make you go places you do not want to go. Your words mean two things, and I do not understand them."

She seemed to think hard, and her reply came as a weak sound. "I'm sorry. I didn't mean to be confusing.... But how in the world could you think of trekking all the way to Ethiopia? And why didn't you tell me about your father's village?"

He said nothing. Since they were married, Leslie had asked him many things that he knew he should not answer.

For a time, they both sat without speaking.

Seeming to forget the argument, she nodded her head in the direction of the vanished Turkana.

"Do you think we run will into any more like them?"

"I cannot say."

She returned to the millet, and after she finished it, the porridge cooked. They ate their meal, and he put up the tent for her.

She held out one of her hands and touched him. "Will you lie with me?"

He smiled. *She thinks of sex. She is no longer angry.*

"I must watch the beasts."

"But you've been walking all night. Don't you need some sleep?"

He smiled again. "With my eyes open, I will rest."

"You can't do that."

She seems playful.

He considered going with her to the tent, but knew he must not. The tradition he knew, the Samburu tradition, told him that he must not have sex with a woman, even a wife, when she is with child. Since he'd found out that Leslie carried the baby, they had argued several times about her desire for sex. More than once he'd surrendered to her, but he'd felt the guilt. In this place, sex would not only be wrong, the distraction would be dangerous.

He told her again of the need to keep watch.

She looked at the sky, showing disappointment. Then she crawled into the tent. She made complaints about the small rocks, and scooping them out, she made a row of piles by the doorway before lying down.

In time, Firingin heard the long breathing of her sleep. He looked and saw that the heifer camel had settled for a rest. The old she-camel stood in the sparse shade of the wind-tattered tree and chewed on her cud. He scanned the horizon and saw no signs of intruders. He closed his eyes and thought of the way he would travel.

It will be northward, but first I will go east toward the Chalbi. If I keep watch for Turkana, maybe, as today, I can hide before we are seen. After a few days, we might see Mount Kulal. Maybe we could go to its high slopes and live a short time there. I could trade my work for food and goods from the nearby Rendille people. If we get close to it, I will speak to Leslie about living on that moun-

tain.

He opened his eyes. Nothing moved—only the slowly waving branch of the overhanging palm and flies swarming on an island of spilled porridge. Away from the shade, sunlight glared from the shimmering desert, the earth baked in the heat.

Again, he let his eyelids close.

Four days Leslie had sat on her high perch and searched the horizons. She'd seen for miles, but not a village had appeared, not another human soul, or anything encouraging. The white sky had glared down, and the rock covered ground had undulated over hills like a scaly reptile. In basins, the land had spilled into alkaline sinkholes, traps where caustic juices dissolved the scales into a sickly bone-yellow. Over everything, the relentless sand had moved, thick or hazy-thin, but always moving.

The camel's motion had become intolerable. Leslie's bottom and her legs had rubbed raw against the carrier. The last two mornings, she'd seen blood on the inside of her wrap. A spot each time, so it probably wasn't serious. Still she worried. How long could a pregnant woman's body take this kind of punishment without consequences?

Wambila had told her that the middle months of a pregnancy were the least critical. "At the end you will be big and awkward," she'd explained, "but during the fourth and fifth months you can do almost anything."

Leslie had asked if that included sex.

"Oh yes, most certainly, even in the ninth month you can... if your husband maintains the interest. Of course, Firingin is from the Samburu. They have strict rules about sex between a man and a pregnant woman."

Leslie and Firingin had made love after she'd told him about the child, but infrequently—not as it had been before. Sometimes, he'd even argued that they shouldn't do it at all, that it was wrong.

The night after the oasis, they'd had intercourse in the open desert with the camels standing and watching. The heat of the argument about the trip must have raised passions enough to overcome Firingin's Samburu restraints.

She was glad it had happened. With the aches and the stiffness of her limbs growing day by day, sex would soon be a thing of the past—until they arrived someplace.

She'd given up on trying to find out where that someplace might be. Firingin didn't know—that was obvious. Maybe when they'd gone far enough, he'd try a Rendille village. Maybe...

Yesterday, her soreness had persuaded her to give walking another try. Firingin had consented after she'd screamed at him about the pain. She couldn't have gone more than a couple of hundred yards when her knees buckled and she'd fallen to the ground. Without a word, he'd picked her up and lifted her back to the seat on the camel.

Like a dynamo Firingin had continued, halting only for evening meals and for a short rest each morning.

After the oasis, he'd prepared all of the food. "It is faster when I do it," he'd said.

If he didn't know where they were going, why was he in such a hurry? She'd asked him, but he'd just looked at her.

Whenever they'd stopped for a meal, he'd put up the tent, so she could stretch out in its shade. He'd cooked, and after they ate, he'd sometimes stood with his body leaning against the hobbled she-camel. Asleep with his eyes open.

Leslie often dozed while riding, but this morning, the fifth of the trip, she was wide-awake and alert.

"With the sunlight," Firingin had said at last night's stop, "I believe there will be another watering hole."

She'd asked him how he knew, and he'd pointed at the ground. "Tracks are many here."

The dot she'd been watching on the horizon grew to become a smudge of olive-green, and she called out to him.

He did not look back.

Thinking he hadn't heard, she raised her voice to give a shout.

He looked at her, and his voice was cold when he spoke.

"You must not yell."

"But you seemed to be going around. I thought you hadn't seen."

"I saw. We will circle the oasis before we approach."

"You think there will be Turkana?"

He stopped the camels, turned and glared at her. "You must keep quiet. If you do not, Turkana or anyone else who is there will hear us."

She answered with silence, and he pulled the camels forward. After a laborious circuit of the grove, a route that climbed rock encrusted hills and crossed several brushy ravines, he led them into the basin. The trees were even more bare than those at the first oasis, but to Leslie the random splotches of shade looked like windows to paradise.

Probably because the old camel was tired, the animal kneeled—a maneuver to help riders dismount, but a technique that brought agony to Leslie's already tortured legs.

"Make her stop!"

Firingin grabbed the lead-rope and gave the command to stand. The creature obeyed, but the upward surge drove new pains into Leslie. Feeling faint, she grabbed at the carrier.

Firingin caught her. He lifted her down and stood as a support until she waved him away. He stepped back, regarding her.

She walked a little, trying to ease the stiffness.

Firingin turned to the task of unloading the camel. Mechanically, as if his mind weren't involved, he marched back and forth, removing items and placing them beside the firepit.

Leslie sat, settling on a pile of blankets beside the bags of supplies.

She started opening containers of cooking utensils.

Flies swarmed, dozens maybe hundreds, drawn by the garbage of previous campers. As if swimming through heavy surf, Leslie flailed her arms at the insects. She hated the flies in Africa.

Firingin unloaded the last of the fodder and spread it over the ground. The camels ate ravenously, the old one carefully placing her hulk between the heifer and the dry feed, and the young creature reaching through legs to get a few morsels.

After standing a time, watching the animals, Firingin went to a nearby thorn bush and cut an armful of twigs. His stamina was unbelievable. Only the coldness in his voice and the tiredness in his eyes showed how near he was to exhaustion.

"This trip, this relentless charge into no-man's land," she muttered to herself, "it's too much, even for him."

Firingin returned to the firepit and stacked his cuttings.

"Don't you want to rest a minute?"

He shrugged, took a pot from the stack of utensils and marched to the watering hole. When he returned, the vessel was filled with a thick and greenish sludge.

He sat the container before her, and she almost gagged.

"You're not thinking of drinking this, are you?"

He looked at her and smiled a smile of forced patience.

"Our water will cook before we drink it."

"Of course. We always boil water, but this isn't water. This is sewage."

His eyes looked through her, as if seeing nothing. "You can strain out the bad part."

She sat, motionless.

"Please strain it," he said. "You know how, do you not?"

She held her breath and poured the slurry through a cloth into a second container. The resulting brew appeared thinner but still greenish in color. She started to pour it out, but Firingin reached and stopped her.

His eyes blazed.

The dirty water issue had grown into a major confrontation.

"Firingin! We can't drink this..."

He held up his hands. "The water we brought with us is gone. We must drink. If we do not, the heat of the desert will make us sick."

She didn't know what to say. After the food poisoning she'd experienced on the trek from Maralal, she knew she couldn't stomach anything that smelled as putrid as this so-called water.

She turned her head and stared at the far horizon.

He placed the pot on the fire and spoke in a voice strained to sound gentle. "If not this, what will you drink?"

"I don't know!" she snapped.

He seemed stunned and said nothing.

"Maybe it's time you bled the heifer."

His eyes opened wide, not angry, but looking at her as if she might be crazy.

"Wambila said you should bleed the heifer every other day. It's so I can have fresh camel's blood to drink. I should have asked you before, but you seemed to be in such a hurry."

"Camel's blood? You wish to drink blood from the camels while we are on the trip?"

"I don't particularly wish to, but I need it for my strength."

Again he raised his hands. "Enough! I cannot bleed the camels. They must keep strong for the traveling."

"But..."

Without warning, he stood and walked away. She saw him gather up the camels' lead ropes, and panic gripped her. He seemed to be leaving.

She yelled for him to wait.

He paid no attention.

Feeling a mounting horror—being abandoned was a nightmare she'd often had since those days of her capture by the Samburu—she struggled to her feet. She hobbled a few steps toward Firingin but stopped when she saw him tie the camels in a shady place under a pair of palm trees.

Still trembling, she watched Firingin return to firepit. He hunkered his body on the other side of the flames and poured boiling liquid from the kettle into the teapot.

While the tea steeped, Firingin and Leslie sat in silence. He poured a cup for himself, and started to drink, and she decided to try a different approach. "The camel's blood is not just for me, you know."

He rolled his eyes and looked away.

"The baby needs it even more than I do. If he doesn't get his protein, he might die inside me."

She knew that Firingin wouldn't know the word protein, but he could understand "child" and "die."

"You don't want your child to die, do you?"

He looked at her for a long moment, and without speaking, he shook his head. He moved to sit beside her, and reached across, touching her abdomen.

Strange man, now his eyes were ringed with tears.

"Your think our child will die?" he said.

She took his hand from her stomach and held his fingers next to her face. He knew so much about caring for cattle and camels and yet so little about the needs of human beings.

He asked about the protein.

"It's something you get from food. Our bodies need it. The baby's body needs much of it to grow and be healthy."

"And you must have camel's blood for this thing?"

She nodded. "Wambila started me on blood weeks ago. She also gave me a bottle for this trip, but I finished it the second day."

He stood and gazed at the camels. "We have many days yet to travel. The beasts will die if I bleed them too soon."

She felt like asking how much farther it would be, but did not. She needed to keep him in this receptive mood.

"Maybe, we ought to stop and rest awhile," she offered. "Sore as I am, a few days staying in one place would be a godsend."

"Maybe, but the fodder is gone. We would need a place where

the animals can find grass."

He sipped at his tea, and after a time, he spoke again. "We will look again at the ravines we saw this morning. Some had trees, and there may be places for grazing."

He scratched the ground with one of the twigs. "The heifer carries a calf. I will not bleed her until she is rested. Before that, you must drink something. If you do not, you will not stay well." She leaned over the pot of steaming tea. The smell could have been worse. She found a cup and poured herself a small portion. She took a sip and waited. A tolerable taste considering.

She smiled. "I'll grind the millet for our breakfast. And, I'll try to grind faster this time."

He nodded.

7

Firingin brought the camels to the campsite and started loading bundles. Leslie stood a distance away, and he noticed that she inspected the cloth of her wrap.

He smiled at her, and she appeared to be embarrassed.

"It's nothing," she said. "Only a small stain."

He thought it strange that she showed embarrassment over a stain in her clothing.

She looked in the bag of bedding and found a sheepskin covering. She had him place it on top of the carrier.

"More padding," she said. "I hope it makes a difference. Otherwise, I may have to walk to the ravine."

He shook his head. Why did she say she would walk when she could not?

Without voicing the question, he lifted her to the seat on the camel and moved the column out to the open desert.

The trek to the first ravine was fast, but just as Firingin remembered from the morning's traverse, the hills around that southwestern opening rose sharply and the passageway was narrow. He decided that the old camel, with her wide load, could not squeeze between the walls.

He led the column farther south to the next ravine. Not much of a distance to travel, but the opening there was also too small. He recalled that there were larger canyons to the north of the oasis.

The sun had risen straight above when the caravan made its way past the watering hole, heading for the northern portals. Firingin suggested a stop for tea.

"Keep going," said Leslie. Tea with water from the oasis spring did not interest her.

They continued, and after another hour, reached the more westerly of the canyons. It had a wide opening—no trouble getting inside, but Firingin would pass it by. He remembered that the large passageway stretched straight and away from the valley. Afternoon winds would bring heat to the open interior from the plains below.

At the second northern ravine he stopped. The entrance was narrow but wider than either of those to the south. High sides cast deep shadows into the chasm. A hopeful feature. Coolness and moisture might lie beyond those shadows.

He led the caravan into the opening.

Between the high walls, the passageway climbed a sharp incline. Leslie moaned against her pain when the old camel's back pitched upward. Knowing that the heifer would bolt if forced to stand where she could not see openness, Firingin did not stop. He pulled the camels forward and hoped that the ravine would not become too narrow. The backing of the young animal from a blocked channel did not make a happy thought for him.

After a long climb, the floor sloped downward and the walls made a sharp turn. Firingin proceeded, and around the corner the pathway leveled and widened. He moved the camels faster, and around another turn the trail led into a small, interior cavern.

Firingin stopped.

He stood, letting his breathing slow to normal. Leslie sat on her perch, rubbing her legs, and the camels fed on tufts of the fresh vegetation. Near the far wall of the cavern, a stand of bamboo grew.

"There will be water in this place."

Leslie said something as an answer. He did not understand the word, but she sounded pleased.

Beyond the bamboo, stood several large leafed trees. He dropped the lead camel's rope and went to inspect.

A few meters from the trees the seeping moisture of a spring pushed through a covering of thick moss.

"Water is coming here."

He reached down and cupped a handful of the liquid. "It is clean and cool. Good for you, and also enough for the camels."

"Fantastic!" Another English word from her.

"It is a blessing from the Gods," he said. "A place not to be expected."

Then came Leslie's voice, harsh with fear.

"Firingin!"

He looked and saw her staring over a tucked shoulder toward a water snake crawling slowly along a ledge of the cavern wall. The creature was not a camel's length from Leslie's face.

Firingin walked to the she-camel and eased her and the heifer toward the middle of the open floor. "Be calm and sit still," he told Leslie.

Scanning the other walls, he saw several lizards and two more snakes. Coolness and the shade had attracted them. He felt disappointment but realized that a camp in the cavern would not be possible.

"We will find a different place for our staying, but first I will fill the water bags and let the camels drink."

Leslie stayed on the old beast while he dumped the smelly liquid from the oasis and dipped fresh spring water into the bags. The camels needed little to drink. After a short time, Firingin picked up the lead-rope and guided the column out of the cavern on an ascending pathway.

The caravan climbed into the open, and after an upward trek of an hour or more, a field of dried grass appeared. He stopped the camels and looked to Leslie.

She said nothing.

The meadow was wide, no ledges where snakes might crawl. The location was remote, not a place where Turkana or Gabbra would be likely to intrude.

He looked at the sky and wondered if police, in their flying machines, might see down.

He spoke the thought to Leslie. She said she did not think he needed to worry about the police.

He looked around the field. Along one side stood a clump of mature thorn bushes. No shade from them, but plenty of wood for a cooking fire. The grass, though dry, had not been uprooted or shredded by winds. Forage would be good for the camels. If there would be no water for the animals, he could take them back to the cavern for their drinking.

"I think we will make our camp here."

She scanned the area. "Won't there be more...?"

He knew her concern. "It will be safe here from snakes. I can make places that are clear of the grass and the bushes."

She smiled. "Good."

He helped her down and handed her the lead rope. "Hold the beasts, and I will make the camp."

She stood, scowling at the clumps of dry vegetation at her feet.

He beat the ground around her. "See, no snakes here, and they will not come to this place." He would tell her those things and hope she wouldn't see any of the creatures.

He unpacked a shovel from the carrier and started to clear the campsite.

The shade extended while he scraped brush and vegetation from a circle more than five camel-lengths across. It would be a wide space where no intruder could approach without being seen. In the morning, he would make another circle for a camp in shadows from the east.

He killed several lizards while he worked. Not the poisonous kind. He and Leslie would eat their flesh for the meal.

After he finished the clearing, he unloaded the rest of the cargo and tied the camels to the thorn bushes.

Leslie stood in the middle of the circle and watched.

He told her it was time to set up the tent, and she handed him the bundle containing the poles and canvas. He erected the structure and spread an awning in front. With collected pebbles, he a made a firepit.

The sun passed behind the hills, and he lit the fire. He piled on wood from the thorn bushes and filled a cooking pot with water for boiling.

It pleased him that the site had few flies. So far from places where people and animals lived, their numbers were small. He removed the knobby skin from the bodies of the lizards and cleaned the gleaming flesh with boiled water.

Leslie's face looked strange, as if she might be ready to cry.

He smiled at her.

"I know," she said. "It tastes like chicken."

He didn't know all the English words she'd used, but her voice sounded agreeable. He nodded and placed the meat on the grate above the coals.

She continued to look strange.

"Pro teen," he said.

She laughed. "I suppose so. But still, it makes my skin crawl."

More words he didn't understand. She did not like the lizards. He knew that. But she laughed. She would eat their meat. The meat of the lizards became white as it cooked. The smell foretold good eating.

Leslie prepared the tea. She did not complain about the water.

When the food was ready, she ate all that he gave her. She also drank of the tea. He enjoyed seeing her eat with pleasure.

From the days of traveling and the work of clearing the campsite, his body ached. He would act as a normal husband and rest under the awning while his wife cleaned up from the cooking and eating.

Darkness came. He sat, and Leslie stayed close. She ate some of her dates.

"When will you draw the blood from the heifer?" she asked.

He did not like her question but would answer without anger. "Not tomorrow. The animal needs to rest."

Drawing blood was a thing he hated to do to his young camel. The beast had never before felt the sting of the arrow. She would be frightened. He wished for the way of the desert, as Hedad had known it. Finding buried tubers under the soil. Bulbs that might bring food for Leslie. Or capturing beetles and other small creatures that she could eat. But such ways, he had learned only a little. His life in the south had taught him only of living with cattle in the mountains.

Leslie crawled into the tent. He heard her spreading the blankets. She came out again. She sat fanning herself with a corner of her wrap.

"It's too hot to sleep."

Without speaking, he nodded. He did not need to say how hot it was.

"So how do you bleed a camel? I never watched when it was done in the village."

He looked away.

The fire made flickering lights on her face. He reached and poured a cup of tea. She held her cup toward him. He filled it.

The two of them sat in front of tent and drank.

She then asked if he'd decided on the place where they would end their trip.

He shrugged and said nothing.

"But you must have thought about it."

"I have thought."

He spoke to her of Mount Kulal.

"How far is it to this mountain?" she asked.

"I think I saw the top of it this morning. It is a peak higher than all the rest. Maybe only another day, maybe two, before we reach the bottom of it, but there would be a climb to the place on the side where we could stay."

"A village, then?"

"No, I think we would live alone there. Mount Kulal is a place where the Rendille people bring their animals for good grass. It is not a place for villages."

"But, I can't have this baby, living alone on a mountain top. I'll need a midwife or somebody to help me when the time comes and before... and after.... Especially after."

He said nothing. It was as he had feared. Leslie would not live on Mount Kulal.

"We should stop at the next village we see," said Leslie.

He shrugged. "I will decide."

She drank, and he watched her. She said no more about stopping at villages.

He told her about the bleeding of the camel. "In the village, it is a task done by two men, maybe more."

"So you can't do it then."

"No, I will do it. I will tie the heifer, so she will be still for it."

She looked into the darkness. "I don't remember any trees around here."

He nodded. "Not here. I cannot bleed the heifer here. I will take her to the green cavern we saw today. There were trees by the spring. I will tie her between two that are strong."

She nodded, but her face looked fearful. He told her that she could stay in the camp while he did the bleeding.

That night, Firingin and Leslie slept together in the tent. Her body remained sore, and she did not want the sex.

He slept without waking until sunlight came into his eyes. Leslie continued to sleep. He made her a cup of tea. Then he started clearing a place for the camp in the eastern shadows. Leslie came out and ground millet for the porridge.

After eating, he moved the tent and then cut an armload of straight branches from the clump of thorn bushes. Two of the longest, he placed in a bath he'd already made by pouring water into a depression in the ground that he had lined with skins. Those staves would soak there until limber. Then he would bind them together with a thong from the tool pack. Notched at both ends, they would be his bow. The bowstring would be the twisted cowhide that was now serving as the front guy for the tent. It had held against the most powerful desert winds. It would be strong enough to launch an arrow a few hand-widths to the bloated vane of the young camel. For the arrows themselves, the straightest branches would be notched and sharpened. He would make two. His biggest task would be the sorting of branches until he found those that would be right.

He sat under the tent's awning sorting and fashioning his arrows. Leslie unpacked and fondled her school supplies.

In the afternoon, he moved the tent to the evening circle and then hunted lizards for the night's meal. He killed six. Enough for a great feast. He moved the camels to fresh grazing and prepared the lizards.

After he and Leslie ate the food and enjoyed the tea, she cleaned the plates and cups and went to bed. He joined her, but they did not sleep. She touched him, and he came to her in the position she called missionary. He felt her belly against his. The baby had grown. He hoped that Nkai would not be angry with their sex.

In the morning, he replaced the tent guy with a strip cloth and told Leslie that he would go to the cavern for the bleeding.

"How long will it take you?"

He shrugged. "Not long. Most of the time will be the going and the coming back. I will take both camels, and I will water them at the spring. On the old one, I will bring back a load of fresh water for our camp."

What she then said surprised him.

"I want to go with you."

His reply came without thinking. "The snakes, they will still be there."

"You can chase them away, can't you?"

"The ones that I see."

"I'll be okay if I stay on the camel.... If she stays in the middle."

He nodded. Water snakes were not the kind that attacked. It was only Leslie's fear that made the trouble. "I will hobble the old beast."

As the caravan entered the cavern, he heard Leslie moan, and he did not know if it was pain or fear that caused her distress. He saw several snakes but they seemed restful.

He tied the legs of Leslie's mount and led the heifer toward the trees. The young beast sensed danger and pulled back on the rope, bawling with a harsh voice. Firingin quieted her by clucking slowly and stroking her face.

He tested a tree near the edge of the grove for strength. The trunk did not bend. He heard no cracking sounds. He looked for a second tree at a proper distance away.

One stood behind a clump of plants. It was farther from the first than he desired, but it appeared strong. He would use the longer rope.

A water snake hung in the tree's lower branches. When he walked toward it, the snake slid into the foliage on the ground. He voiced apologies and tried the tree's strength. It was as strong as the first. He looked at Leslie. She had her eyes closed. The she-camel grazed on the grass.

He took a breath. The next part would not be to his liking.

He tied the heifer's lead rope to the first tree and fastened one end of the longer rope as a binding for the creature's hind legs. He used a regular hobble on the legs in front.

The animal bawled again.

He looped the long rope around the trunk of the second tree and started pulling. The heifer's voice rose to a high pitch. She cried until her hind legs lifted from the ground. Then, she fell on her side, and the bawling stopped.

Firingin stretched the rope tight, pulling the heifer between the two trees. With the tension on her body, the frightened animal resumed her crying.

He left her and walked to the she-camel.

"She sounds terrible," said Leslie.

He nodded and unpacked the bow and one of the two arrows. Taking a gourd to catch the blood, he returned to the heifer.

He tightened a short segment of rope around the animal's neck, making the large vane bulge with the pressure. The heifer flailed her legs, tearing up grass and throwing sticks.

Firingin took aim from close range and fired the arrow into the jugular. The animal coughed and squealed. Blood pumped in a thin stream from its neck.

Firingin grabbed the collecting vessel, and leaned close to the frightened eyes of the beast. He spoke soft words into the ears.

The gourd filled, and Firingin quickly released the neck rope. He slapped a handful of mud over the oozing wound and tied a wrap of cloth over the mud.

Holding the container of blood in his hands, he turned to show it to Leslie.

He did not see her!

He untied the heifer and frantically scanned the area.

Leslie and the she-camel were gone!

The pain in Leslie's legs seemed to have eased. Maybe after a few days rest and then getting some strength from the camel's blood, she'd be ready to go again. Firingin had told her about a mountain where he wanted to live. Two days from here, he'd said. But how could they possibly live alone on a mountain top?

Firingin had also told her about the bleeding of the heifer. He'd said he'd go to the green place to do it. She didn't see how she could go back there—with snakes crawling everywhere.

In the darkness, the air cooled fast. She finished her tea and for the second time crawled into the tent.

A little less of a furnace now. She removed her wrap and felt for blood. It felt moist. Maybe it was an open sore from the ride up the canyon. Rough as it was, there could have been something. Tomorrow, in daylight, she would check again. If the blood was still there she'd have to tell Firingin about it. Not that she knew what he could do after she told him—no way to call a medi-vac even if there was one. Summoning help of any kind would probably be a sure way of bringing the police.

She tried to think of something different. The evening meal came to mind and she smiled.

Imagine him using the word protein when he wanted me to eat the lizard meat.

Firingin crawled into the tent. He seemed aroused but didn't try to come to her.

The following morning, Firingin got up before she did. She slept in the cool hours until he came smiling into the tent with a cup of tea in his hands.

"It will be our day for resting," he said.

She thought of sex, but wanted first to check for the bleeding. She waved him away and inspected herself and the blankets. A couple of spots on the cloth, not big. It probably was irritation from the ride yesterday.

She looked outside and saw that Firingin had gone to the shady side of the field. There he scraped a place in grass for moving the camp. She got dressed.

For the breakfast, she ground millet. When Firingin took a break, they ate their meal. He then finished clearing the circle, and she cleaned the dishes.

He started making the bow and the arrows he would use for bleeding the camel. She sat under the awning and looked through her school supplies. The pencils needed sharpening. She worked on them awhile and then turned through a stack of tablets. Drawings left on the top pages reminded her of the day when the police came.

She thought of the story about the Ohio dairy she'd started to tell her students—a story they had loved. Then they'd heard the whopping of the helicopters.

She put away the school supplies and let her eyes close. She must try to forget about that dreadful day and think of the future. She needed to imagine a place where she and Firingin might live their lives again. She needed to but she couldn't. In this northern country, busy villages like Jeiso's did not seem to exist. How could she have friends and start a school when there weren't any people? By the time Firingin had finished his work on the arrows and the bow, the sun had moved to western hills. He moved the camp and then started supper.

The main course was, again, broiled lizard. For dessert, Leslie ate the rest of her dates. She offered some to Firingin, but he shook his head. He never ate dates. She went early to the tent and checked herself for blood. None this time. She waited for Firingin.

The day of resting must have made him passionate. When he came to the tent, he was ready, and in spite of his Samburu inhibitions, they made wonderful love and then slept like babies.

In the morning he told her that he would go to bleed the heifer. "You can wait, here," he added.

She asked how long he'd be gone.

He answered that it wouldn't be long.

He talked, then, of taking both camels.

She'd be marooned!

She remembered the night she'd stayed alone near Parsaloi and how terrifying it had been.

"I want to go with you."

His eyes widened with surprise. He spoke of the snakes. She asked if he couldn't scare them away.

He said he could if he saw them. His eyesight was good, much better than hers. She told him that she would sit on the camel in the middle of the cavern. He said he would hobble the creature there.

After placing the heavy blanket on the carrier, he raised her to the perch.

No pain on the ride down until the braking on the final slope took its toll. Her bruises were all renewed by the constant sliding and steep pitching.

Inside the grotto she looked for snakes. The light could have been better, but she saw none.

Firingin lead the old camel to the center and hobbled her.

"You will have nothing to fear," he said.

To be sure she wouldn't see something that would make her scream, Leslie closed her eyes. She would keep them closed until Firingin was back at her side.

Presently, she heard the heifer bawling. The poor thing was terrified. The old camel moved under Leslie. A short hopping motion, traveling only a foot or two.

Firingin's voice came, talking low and sing-songy. She couldn't make out what he said, but hoped it wasn't one of his prayers to a snake.

The young heifer let out another bellow and then squealed. Firingin kept talking.

After a time, he came to the old camel. Leslie watched while he removed things from the carrier. She closed her eyes when he left.

The heifer wailed louder than ever, coughing and gurgling. Leslie kept her eyes closed.

The old camel bawled, hopping sideways several times. Leslie hung on with both hands. The camel kept moving. The movement felt as if the animal were loose. Leslie opened her eyes and saw that the camel was no longer in the cavern.

"Whoa," she shouted. "Whoa, you crazy fool."

The camel paid no attention.

The path ahead narrowed, brush on both sides. The hill sloped sharply downward.

"Oh God!"

The camel started braking against the grade but couldn't seem to stop.

With surprising agility, considering her sore body, Leslie threw her left leg over the top of the carrier and launched herself toward the rocky bank.

The camel gave a buck, causing Leslie to fly, feet-first, over a thorn bush alongside the path and onto a bed of hard shale. Wind knocked out of her, Leslie laid on her side. Blood oozed from her elbows and her knees.

She tried to stand, but once on her feet, she felt the stab of numbing pain in her right ankle. She looked down and saw the foot bent over at a grotesque angle.

She sat down hard.

She rolled her body from behind the bushes and saw the camel.

The creature had continued a distance down the slope, and there it stood, looking back as if to say: "You idiot, why did you jump?"

Leslie tried once more to get to her feet.

Too much pain.

She closed her eyes to hold back the panic.

Why doesn't Firingin come?

Maybe he doesn't even know I'm gone. Maybe he's still doing the bleeding.

She started yelling.

The camel walked slowly up the canyon, grazing on patches of dried grass.

Leslie tried to crawl.

The incline was too steep.

She yelled again. Then she saw Firingin leading the heifer and running down the hill.

She waved her arms, but he'd already seen her.

"Are you hurt?" he shouted.

"Yes, and I can't walk."

He came to where she sat. "I am so happy to find you." He took her in his arms—a thing he almost never did unless they were making love.

She felt tears come.

"The camel got loose and went by herself," she blubbered.

"Yes, it is my fault. I should have hobbled her better."

"I had my eyes closed and didn't..."

"I did not know you were gone. The heifer cried so loud I did not hear."

Seeming, then, to remember that the young animal was with him, he stood and tied the creature to a thorn bush.

"Can you stand?" he asked Leslie.

"I can't put my weight on the right foot. The ankle is sprained I think."

He looked hard at the bent-over ankle. He said nothing.

He brought the old camel to Leslie.

"Use my shoulder and try to raise yourself up."

Leslie pulled herself to where she could stand, leaning against him.

"Do you think you can you ride?"

"Yes, I think so. I can't walk, that's for sure."

He lifted her to the carrier. Her ankle hung down, limp. He examined it with both hands.

"I do not think a bone is broken."

His fingers made her wince, but she said nothing.

"When we arrive at the camp, I will wrap the leg between sticks of wood."

She smiled. "So, you're a doctor too!"

Looking sheepish, he shrugged. He steadied Leslie with one hand and tied the heifer behind the she-camel.

"What about the camel-blood?" asked Leslie.

He smiled. "It is in the gourd. I put the gourd on a big rock before I came to look for you. It will be there."

She wiped away the tears, and she smiled. "I can hardly wait."

At sunrise Firingin made ready to leave the camp. Loud and with much screaming, Leslie had talked all through the night. The swelling of her ankle had made her hot inside her body. She complained that she was on fire. Yet in the morning's sunlight, she shivered and asked for blankets. He brought coverings to her, but she soon threw them off.

He boiled water, and when it cooled, he squirted mouthfuls on her face and neck. It helped only a little.

For three days she'd been sick. The heat in her body had grown, and now Firingin feared that in one more day, maybe two, she would die from it.

He took the tent apart. Leslie shivered on the blankets while he loaded equipment along with what remained of the food. Two days ago he had thrown out the camel's blood. Leslie had consumed but a small part of it.

Using poles of the tent and its fabric, he built a platform for Leslie. He tied it on top of the carrier, and when all was ready, he lifted her up. She would ride lying down with wraps of cloth tied around her legs and waist.

He considered searching for a more gentle route to the valley floor, one that would go around the back of the hills. The ride for

Leslie might be easier that way, but much time would be wasted in finding such a trail. They would go down on the pathway he knew, the one through the green cavern. At the spring, he would stop and fill the water bottles. The camels would have a short drink, and he would splash cooling liquid over Leslie. They would then go to the oasis and look for a well-traveled trail northward. Still in Rendille country, most of the traffic would lead to friendly villages, places where help might be found.

He shook his head as he thought of his hopes for passing through this region without bringing police danger to the people—hopes that he must now abandon.

The old camel braked her way down the trail toward the cavern. Firingin looked back at Leslie and saw that she slept. Her head flopped from one side to the other as the camel walked. Firingin wished for more comfort for Leslie but would not tie wraps around her head. Scanning skyward, he saw that high clouds had moved across the sun. The day would be cooler. He mouthed a prayer of thanks.

Near midday the column made its way across the broad valley and, once again, approached the oasis. Firingin surveyed the area and saw no visitors other than a flock of scavenging vultures. He led the camels to the watering hole and lifted Leslie down.

He splashed gourds of the water from the well onto her body. She waved her arms, complaining. He continued. If he could cool her, even for a short time, it might keep her breath from fading into gasps and wheezes.

Her eyes opened, and she sat up.

"Pew. What is that stuff?"

He poured more water on her legs. "It is to cool you. We are at the oasis."

She made a gagging sound and reached for the gourd. With surprising strength, she knocked the vessel out of his hands.

He smiled. "You are better."

"I am wet, covered with stinking wet stuff."

She wiped her hands over her self. "I can't believe you'd pour that sewage all over me."

Pleased with her show of vitality, he smiled again.

"We will go now."

He lifted her back on the camel, and selecting a route along a track heavy with prints of men and camels, he moved the column northward.

Leslie moaned and sometimes cried out, but other than a look to be sure she hadn't fallen, Firingin did not divert his eyes from the pathway ahead.

The route he had taken continued to abound with signs of travelers, yet it seemed to lead nowhere. Hours passed and no settlement appeared.

The sun set and the westerly winds blew. In the darkness the gusts seemed to bring fright to Leslie. She screamed aloud, and one of her sounds came so fierce it made the heifer-camel bolt and tear lose from the rope.

Firingin pulled the she-camel to a halt. He would make a camp so Leslie could lie in shelter until the heifer decided to come back.

He helped Leslie down and used a blanket to make a tent for her. He ground a handful of millet. The smell of mashed grain would entice the wayward camel.

He waited.

The young animal moved from the shadows and stood a short distance from the camp. She sniffed toward the millet. Firingin clucked to ease her fear. When she came to him, he placed a hand on her halter. He tied her to the hobbled she-camel, crawled into the makeshift tent and laid his body beside Leslie.

Heat rose from Leslie's skin. He poured water from a carrying bag and splashed the liquid over her face. She breathed easier and slept.

After midnight the wind quieted, and he took down the blanket-tent and packed it. When he raised Leslie to the carrier, she flopped, limp and heavy against him. He heard her whimper and only by that did he know that she was not dead.

The trek continued, and in time the trail widened. The mass of

a large mountain loomed in the west—Mount Kulal, he thought.
He considered another stop. Leslie could lie on the unmoving
ground while he decided if they should abandon their searching for
unseen villages and take refuge on a high, cool slope.

He slowed the caravan and, in the distance, he heard the bark of
a dog. His heart pounding, he turned the camels toward the sound
and, after a short march to the crest of a nearby hill, he saw a wide
valley stretching toward the base of the mountain. Nearby, in the
valley, was a collection of dwellings circled as a Rendille settlement.

He looked to the sky and gave thanks to the Gods. He turned
to tell Leslie of their good fortune, but Leslie continued to sleep.

He hunkered in front of the camels to wait for daylight. It
would not be wise to approach a desert community in darkness.

He saw two figures emerge from behind a fence that guarded
the village corral, sentries coming to investigate. One walked ahead.
The other followed with raised spear. Below the hill where Firingin
held his camels, they stopped.

"Name yourself," shouted the sentry ahead.

Firingin stood and answered in a loud voice, "I am a kinsman.
Firingin, first grandson of Jeiso Hedaidile."

The second warrior started to lower his spear, but a word from
his companion and he raised it again.

"Lead your beasts forward," said the leader.

Firingin obeyed, stopping his animals two lengths in front of
the warriors.

The older one's eyes moved from Firingin to the rear of the
column and back to Firingin.

"Hedaidile," he said. "I know the name. But why are you, his
grandson, here? And so early before daylight?"

Firingin tilted his head toward Leslie on the carrier. "My woman
and I travel far. She is fevered and needs care."

The warrior behind now planted his spear in the ground. The
first spoke again to Firingin. "The headman sleeps. I will not wake
him for one with such a strange story."

Leslie cried out, as if in a dream. Her words were in English.

Both warriors raised their weapons.

Leslie screamed. The younger warrior ran and took shelter behind an anthill. The first stood his ground but looked fearful. "You have brought a demon into our midst!"

"No, no. She is my wife. She speaks strange, but she is not evil."

The warrior looked toward the village and toward his companion behind the anthill. He spoke rapidly to the younger. Firingin could not make out the words, but the second warrior abandoned his hiding place and came forward.

The first warrior spoke with a harsh voice to Firingin. "You must wait here. When the headman wakes, I will speak with him. He will decide on this."

He then walked back toward the corral. The other stayed, his eyes bright with fear.

Firingin wondered what the headman's decision might be. Jeiso's name had drawn a favorable response, but Leslie's demon-cries may have frightened all the good favor away.

The lone guard sat on his haunches. It seemed the wait would be long. Firingin proceeded to remove the wraps from Leslie's limbs and to ease her down from the camel.

He placed her body on the ground and used the rest of the spring water to cool her.

He looked toward the eastern horizon. A pink glow above the dark hills announced the sun's arrival. A sky the color of bright blossoms, an omen for a day of strong winds. He hoped that Leslie would have shelter before the winds came.

The top of the tall mountain glistened and the light of the sun moved slowly down the sides. Sounds of the waking village filled the air: complaining voices as women and children emerged from dwellings for morning chores; bleating of goats being moved from pen to pen for the milking. A rooster crowed, and dogs yelped and snarled through their first fight of the day.

The noises brought memories of Firingin's former home, the place in the south where he had lived as the eldest son of Jeiso's eldest daughter, the Samburu village where he grew to the size of a man but lived as a child. It was a place he hated, but a place with sounds that he had loved.

He sat himself on the ground close to Leslie. He inspected her injured leg.

The swelling had grown and the color had darkened to a shade of purple. He fixed his gaze on the village and prayed for the awakening of its headman.

The sun climbed and shadows shortened in the wadi. The hunkered guard fell asleep.

Firingin sat and stroked Leslie's face.

The sun had moved far overhead when a man came walking with the elder warrior.

Firingin stood.

The man had the step of a leader, but his dress was plain. Other than metal jewelry in his ear lobes, he wore nothing but a wrap of bleached cloth around his lower body and boxlike hat on the back of his head.

As the pair drew near, Firingin saw the man's eyes. They gleamed bright with curiosity—a favorable sign.

The young sentry shook off his sleep and stood. His spear, he lifted to the position of a salute.

The new man spoke. "Where is this one, the demon who so frightens my sentries?"

The warrior pointed to Leslie who still laid on the ground. "She is there. The woman who speaks a strange tongue and brings forth the cries of a hunting hyena."

The man in white leaned toward Leslie and scowled.

Firingin came to stand before him and tried to speak with a confident voice. "This woman talks with strange words, and she screams, but she does so because of a fever she has. She does not mean to frighten your..."

The elder held up a hand for silence. He stepped around Firingin, and his eyes moved back to Leslie. As if a cat inspecting its prey, he stared at her.

"This woman is not Rendille."

Firingin stood silent. He considered telling the headman the story: that Leslie was a white woman sought by police, and that she now traveled with Firingin northward, seeking safety.

He considered it, but he would not speak of such things. If Leslie lived, Firingin would soon take her away from this place. If she did not live, he would leave alone. In either case, the village of this headman would be better not to know of the police.

"The women is pale of color," said Firingin. "But she is my wife. She carries my child in her belly."

"And you are Jeiso Hedaidile's first grandson?"

"I am. Firingin is my given name."

"A Samburu name!"

Firingin nodded. The headman had wisdom beyond his years.

"I was a child in the land of the Samburu. My mother took me there to live in the village of her husband."

The elder looked back toward his own village.

"I have heard this story." He looked at Leslie with great intensity then back to Firingin.

"Our spirit man is old, but he has many skills. Skills I do not understand. I will send men, and they will carry your woman to him."

A Laidetidetan, thought Firingin, a diviner, or even a Milkika, an evil spirit man. Such a personage should not care for Leslie. He voiced his concern.

The headman looked up, his eyes hard. "Gof is the healer for our village. He will see to this woman, or she will die before the sun passes to the western hills. Even now, her breath is short."

Firingin had great fear of the evil ones of spirit, but he could not let Leslie die because of his fear.

Shutting his eyes, he nodded. "Take her to him."

Two men from the village carried Leslie to a hut that stood isolated from the others—the dwelling of Gof, the healer.

Firingin followed the bearers and would have gone inside the dwelling, but he was stopped at the doorway.

"You will stay in the corral," said the headman. "There you will pay for the care of your woman by helping with the beasts, and you will eat and sleep with the herders."

Firingin didn't mind caring for beasts or living with herders, but he had concern for Leslie. He voiced his protest and saw warriors moving toward him. They menaced with their spears, and the headman again told Firingin to leave.

Each day, Firingin did his work in the corrals during the morning and evening hours. The afternoons he spent sitting where he could see the dwelling of the one named Gof.

As days passed to three and four, he sat waiting but was not allowed entry. He sat and he hoped for the time when he and Leslie would be gone from this place.

He thought again of Mount Kulal. Visible, and close in the west, its high slopes lay dark and tempting.

Firingin did not converse with the people of the village, or wish to be known by them. Neither did the people seem interested in conversation with him. Even in the corral he worked away from the others. It is better, he thought.

Gof told him nothing until the afternoon of the fifth day. On that day, the healer came to the place where Firingin sat.

"The woman is no longer in danger of dying," said Gof.

The brief announcement so pleased Firingin that he jumped to his feet and ran toward the dwelling. The man of spirits moved as a gazelle and blocked the doorway.

Gof spoke with words more fierce than his appearance. "You must not enter," he said. "If you do, you will bring a curse on her. A curse that would threaten her life. It is a curse that will come also to you, if you try again."

Such threats from one so powerful distressed Firingin. He needed to think about their meaning. He left Gof and returned to the corral.

The following morning, as Firingin did his chores, he heard other herders talking. One of them spoke of an assault on the village by Kenyan police, an attack that had happened only a few days before Firingin's arrival. The words brought great concern to Firingin. He held his breath to hear more, but the talking stopped. He approached the young man who'd been speaking and asked him about the police raid. The question brought fear to the herder's eyes, and he denied any knowledge of the police.

Believing that the man kept secrets and the police might return to the village, Firingin ran to Gof's dwelling. He would demand to see Leslie and would warn her of the danger. If she were strong enough to travel, they would leave at once.

Gof sat by his doorway, grinding herbs.

"I would speak with her," said Firingin.

Gof blinked. "You cannot. This I have already told you."

"You must allow me. I have heard a thing that I must warn her about."

The paint on Gof's face cracked with his grin. "What have you heard? What is it you must speak of?"

"The police. They have been in this village. I have heard it said in the corral. I fear their return."

A silence grew, and even from behind the paint and feathers, Gof's eyes showed great trepidation.

Firingin looked hard into the countenance.

"Your curse cannot stop me," he said. "I will see for myself of my woman's strength for travel."

He moved toward the doorway, but Gof reached across with one of his arms. The healer spoke with a quiet voice and said compromising words: "Your woman sleeps, but I will allow you to see her when she wakes."

Firingin smiled. His boldness had overcome this spirit man and his curses.

"But you, grandson of Hedaidile," added Gof, "you will not speak of the police when you see her."

"I must speak of them. They bring danger to her."

Gof held up his hands as a protest. "It is danger she must not hear of."

"It is danger she must hear of. We must leave this place."

"Your woman is with child."

Firingin nearly laughed in the healer's face.

"The woman's condition is known to me."

Gof nodded. "You know that much... but you do not know how loosely the child is held in her."

Firingin said nothing. He knew little of the way babies were carried inside a woman.

"If you tell your woman of the terror of police in this village, I fear that she too will wish to leave. Such leaving would loosen her body's grip on the infant. The child will be born dead. A curse on your child, but also on your woman. A curse not from me, young Hedaidile, but from you."

Firingin shuddered at the fearsome words.

"I will wait by your dwelling until she wakes," he said.

Gof nodded and pointed to a place for Firingin to sit beside the doorway.

10

Leslie opened her eyes and saw him, and fully awake for the first time in days, she stared blankly at the personage beside her. A man, for certain, but all covered with feathers, his face and arms festooned with white and black designs.

Nobody she knew, but his image seemed familiar, part of a mixture of images her fevered brain had dealt with over the last... last how long? She had no idea how many days she'd been here.

Trying Swahili, she asked, "Who are..."

The feathered man scowled at her, or a least it looked like a scowl, and he held up a hand for silence.

She obeyed.

He returned to staring at the dirt floor, intent, it seemed, on analyzing an array of small bones and bits of fur and skin. Leslie could see nothing in the items that so captivated her bedside companion. She looked beyond them and saw the stark, interior walls of a native dwelling. She must be in a village, but where? And where was Firingin?

The feathered one swept up his collection and deposited it in a skin pouch at his waist. He smiled, stained teeth signaling joy from the painted face, but he said nothing.

Leslie spoke Firingin's name. It produced a nod of recognition from the feathered one. He crawled to the doorway and spoke to someone outside.

The someone entered. It was Firingin. He must have been waiting by the entrance.

"Hello," he said. "You are awake."

"Obviously."

He didn't seem to understand.

She clarified. "Yes, I am."

He sat near her. The feathered man nodded once and left the dwelling.

Leslie stared at the vacant entryway. "Who was that..." She felt like saying, "masked man," but Firingin definitely wouldn't have understood that. "...Who was that character?"

Smiling, Firingin answered. "That one is Gof, the spirit man of this village. He has saved your life, I think."

"A witch doctor?"

Firingin looked puzzled. "Witch doctor? I do not know what that means."

"Like you said, a spirit man. But, he couldn't have saved my life. I only had a fever and..."

He held up a hand. "You are better."

"Yes, I suppose so. The fever is gone, anyway."

She looked at her previously swollen ankle. "And my ankle looks almost normal, again."

Firingin nodded. "So, it is true. Gof has fixed you."

"How could he? All I've seen him do is look at pieces of animal bone and skin on the floor."

"He has fed you good food, and he uses herbs. He grinds the herbs outside. I have seen him do it."

"I don't remember eating, but... Herbs you say?"

Firingin nodded.

"Well, that makes sense."

She rolled onto her elbow and sat up.

Firingin appeared concerned. "You must not do too much."

"I feel well enough to sit and talk."

He smiled an uncertain smile.

"So, how long have I been in this place?"

"Six days we have been in this village."

"And you're probably itching to leave... Where are we, anyhow?"

He nodded toward the doorway. "We are by Mount Kulal. It is outside to the west of here. But..." He looked at her for a long moment and then spoke again. "There has been trouble, Leslie."

She waited for him to continue. Waited and hoped that the trouble he spoke of wouldn't force them to return to the desert. Even with a witch doctor running the local clinic, this was a community of human beings, a place where she would like to stay, find friends, maybe start a school.

Firingin remained silent.

"Trouble?" she prompted. "What kind of trouble?"

He didn't answer. He looked again toward the doorway. Clearly, he did not want to talk about the subject he'd just raised.

She tried once more to motivate him. "So...."

He kept staring toward the outside.

"So, are we going to stay here then?"

He looked at her sharply. "I cannot say more."

She reached for his arm. "What is..."

His glare stopped her in mid-sentence. "I should not have spoken of it." He looked away then crawled out through the doorway.

"What in the world is going on here?" She rocked to her knees to go after him. She moved off the bedmat, but before she reached the exit, the feathered man appeared and placed his body in front of her.

"Shit!"

Keeping between her and the opening, the witch doctor filled a cup with a grayish liquid from a gourd snatched from a row by the wall.

The smell of him, or perhaps the liquid, almost gagged her.

He backed her to the bedmat, holding the cup toward her. He smiled, nodding for her to drink.

When she could back no farther, she pursed her lips tight and shook her head from side to side.

The feathered man's smile faded to a terrifying stare, and he ground his teeth at her.

Petrified, she relented and took a small sip.

Slowly, the feathered man's smile returned.

Leslie did not see it. She was already asleep.

11

Distressed after his fractured talk with Leslie, Firingin walked away from Gof's dwelling and toward the village corral.

He thought, as he walked, of what he'd said to Leslie and of what he hadn't said. He'd wanted to speak to her of the police danger and the need to leave this place. He'd wanted to, but as soon as he'd started, he'd thought of Gof, sitting outside. Fear of Gof's curse had stopped the words before he could even speak them. Vowing not to try saying more to Leslie until he knew all about the police raid, he changed his direction of walking. He would go to the village courtyard, and there he would look for the one he had not seen since his first day in the settlement, the man with the box-hat, the head elder.

In the open area at the center of the community, many men were gathered, talking and playing bau. In one of the groups, the man Firingin sought conversed with several others.

Firingin stopped a distance away.

The talkers had much to say to each other about many things: the grazing season that would soon start; caravan problems—all villages had problems with their camel and cargo trade; and the Turkana—the warriors from beyond the lake had been busy in this part of the desert.

Firingin waited and said nothing.

Some of the men in the circle stared at him. A number stopped talking and left. In time, the group reduced to only four. The headman held up a hand and looked at Firingin.

"What is it you want?"

The remaining elders stared, waiting for Firingin's answer.

"I wish to know about the attack on this village by Kenyan police."

The headman's eyes brightened with concern and he waved the others away.

They grumbled but dispersed as ordered.

The headman waited a time, then asked, "Where did you hear of such attack?"

Firingin shrugged. "It does not matter. I heard and now I wish to know what you say of it."

The headman scowled. "I will find out who spoke to you", he said. "The disobedience of my orders will not go unpunished."

Firingin felt the fire of anger. "You do not need to find the one who told me. He spoke it to another, and I only heard his words from a distance. He would not speak them straight to me. When I asked Gof about the raid, his eyes showed great fear and he too told me nothing. I come to you because I must know if the Kenyan police have been here, as I have heard. If they have attacked this village. And, if they have asked questions."

He waited, expecting a response, but the head elder said nothing.

"I have a concern about the police, and I must know if I and my woman must make haste to leave this place."

The headman breathed a deep breath. "I know you have a concern, but you do not need to leave here in haste. I have told no one that you are the ones the soldiers sought."

Firingin stared, astounded.

"You know that we are the ones they look for?"

The headman nodded. "While his soldiers destroyed dwellings

and ran off camels, the Kenyan officer told me in English that they searched for a white woman and a man who had escaped from Jeiso Hedaidile's settlement. He said the man had a Samburu name. He said that name to me, and I knew, for I have heard the story of your mother and how she had a Rendille son in Samburu country, that the man was the great Hedaidile's number one grandson."

"You knew that, and you keep it a secret from the people of your village. Why?"

"The devastation here was great and there is much anger. I cannot allow such anger to be directed toward the family of Hedaidile. The Rendille people have many enemies: the Turkana, the Gabbra and others. We must not make enemies of each other."

"You use big words, and I understand your meaning. But why did you not turn us away when you saw us standing in the desert?"

The headman looked to the sky and back to Firingin. "When my warrior first told me of you, that same grandson of Hedaidile, here with a strange woman, I wanted to tell him to send you away, back to the sand and the wind.... I wanted to, but I could not. I saw the hand of Wak in your arrival at our village—a test for me and my people, a test that would not be met by a show of weakness."

Firingin felt sadness for the trouble he had brought to this man.

"But I will tell you now, young Hedaidile," added the headman, "if the police return while you are here, I will lead them to you. I cannot risk the destruction they would bring if I said nothing and they discovered you in our midst."

Firingin felt an overpowering need to explain. "My woman was sick. She..."

The elder raised a hand.

"I must tell you one more thing. I cannot be responsible for the safety of you or of your wife if you tell this thing to any of my people."

Firingin shook his head. "You do not need to be, as you say, responsible. We will go. Gof says Leslie will not die. I will take her, and we will leave your village on this day."

The headman's eyes widened. "You cannot. Your woman may not die, but she is not well. Gof tells me that she is with child, and that the child is not tight in her body. She cannot travel."

Firingin marveled at the headman's knowledge of all things in his village but spoke objection to what the headman had said.

"We traveled far before we came to you. Leslie carried the child without trouble. The danger we bring to your people is too great. We will go from here."

The headman stared toward Gof's dwelling. "I, myself, have a special worry. My healer has said that the child your wife carries is a male. It will be an important heir of the Hedaidile family, a great-grandson to Jeiso. If I let you take the woman, and the child is born dead, Wak will see, and in time, others will know. My village would soon be cursed by all the clans in the south. The burden of curses from so many would be great, much greater than that of waiting the days until your woman is well enough to travel."

Firingin nodded. The headman's mind worked as that of a leader. It would be foolish to continue the battle of words with such a person. Perhaps the fears are false. Many days might pass before the police return.

He asked the head elder if he had heard of helicopter raids on other settlements.

"Only on your grandfather's community. The Kenyan officer told me that he had been there two times with his flying machines. The second time, Jeiso was taken."

"Taken!"

"Yes, taken to a Kenyan jail in the city of Nakuru. The officer spoke of the fight old Hedaidile had made with his knife, a good fight but no match for the power of the Kenyan soldiers."

Firingin felt weakness in his legs. Jeiso fighting with the knife and now gone.

"I must find him..."

The headman shook his head. "You cannot. Nakuru is far to the south of here."

"I must," said Firingin, and he left the headman standing.

Past dwellings, Firingin walked as in a dream until he stood at the edge of the desert. There, facing southward, he thought about what he would do.

In his life he had learned little of the ways of a man, but he did know one thing well. Any one who would call himself a man could not leave another, especially his own grandfather, to suffer for things he, himself, had done.

Firingin knew he must go to free Jeiso, and he also knew he must go without Leslie.

She cannot travel. Gof who knows of such things, has said that she must rest or the baby will not stay in her. Days might pass while she rests, days that Jeiso would suffer in the prison.

Firingin knew he would miss Leslie's smiles and her funny ways. I will be gone for many round moons, he thought. I might never see her again. I might be killed when I try to free Jeiso, or the Kenyans might put me in jail for my life. He thought of Leslie living alone. What if the baby is born dead? Leslie will grieve. It saddened him to think of her grieving, without family or friends to give her comfort. Perhaps, on his trip to the south, he would stop at Jeiso's village and tell them where Leslie stayed. In time, if he did not return, someone from there could come for her. But she would need care for her living until they came.

Firingin walked back to the courtyard. He would talk again to the headman. He would ask him to give Leslie a place for living until he returned or until Jeiso's people came.

In the central plaza, a number of elders played games and talked, but the village leader was not among them. Firingin sat where he and the headman had talked, and he waited.

The sun dipped low in the west, and the man Firingin waited for did not appear. The sounds of evening chores came from the corral, and Firingin knew he must go and help. But first he would visit Gof's dwelling and demand to see Leslie.

The spirit man rose to greet him and held up a feathered arm.

"I must talk to her," said Firingin.

"The woman sleeps. She will not be awake before tomorrow's

sunrise."

Firingin voiced his frustration. "You must wake her. Use your powers, your herbs."

"I will let you see her tomorrow," said the healer and sat himself in the entrance of his dwelling. Satisfied with that, Firingin continued to the corral. He did his work and after the animals were fed and bedded, he sat, alone by the fence.

I will go early and talk to Leslie, he thought, but how will I tell her what I have to say? She will be angry when I say that I must go to free Jeiso, but I will not hide from her anger. She will want to know when I will return, but I cannot tell her that thing. If I had talked to the headman about her care, I could have told her what he said. Now I will have to guess at his generosity.

Firingin thought of what he might offer as payment for Leslie's care. His only possessions were the heifer and the few goods taken for the trip. He could give up the heifer but he needed the goods for his trek to free Jeiso.

He thought of the way he would save Jeiso. He knew he could not fight the Kenyan police. I will go to them, he thought, and I will tell them that I am the one they seek. Then Jeiso will be freed. He thought of South Horr. He had seen police on the streets of South Horr, a town not two weeks away. I will walk to that place to give up myself, and I will stop at Jeiso's village on the way.

Tired of thoughts and questions, Firingin went to his camels. They were asleep, and he laid down beside them. He listened to their gentle breathing, and in time he also slept.

12

The feathered man left, and Firingin came and sat be side Leslie. A harried look showed in Firingin's eyes.

"You appear well," he said.

"Better, I think, but still confused."

She waited for him to respond.

He didn't.

"So, what is it you didn't want to talk about last time?"

He rubbed a hand over his mouth.

She waited.

After a time, he spoke. "The headman..."

"Yes, the headman?"

Firingin nodded. "The headman of this village talks to me."

Again, Firingin had stopped short of making any sense.

"Yes, yes," she urged, "what does this headman say to you?"

Firingin drew a breath and held it a moment. Then he blurted, "The police, they have been to this place."

She said nothing.

"They were here on a day before we came," Firingin added.

"Looking for us, I suppose?"

He nodded.

She continued. "And, I guess they came with their helicopters and soldiers... wrecking everything? Throwing..."

Firingin held up a hand. "Please, Leslie."

She smiled a tentative smile.

"The headman says his people are angry."

"I can imagine."

"He says we must not tell them that we are the ones the police came for."

"But..."

"The Kenyans only talked to the headman and he has not told his people what they said."

"I see...."

Firingin had started looking toward the doorway with a gaze so intense, Leslie lifted her eyes to see what might be there.

Nothing.

"Did the police say they'd been back to Jeiso's?" She hoped the question might break Firingin's trance.

She waited, and then she answered herself.

"I guess they had, or else they wouldn't have known we'd left. Shit, what do we do now?"

No reply.

She leaned as far as she could into his field of view. "What is wrong, my husband?"

She waited, and after a time, he looked at her. The look in his eyes had changed from haggard to one of enormous sadness.

"Jeiso is gone," he said.

"Gone? What do you mean? He's not...?"

Seeing the grief in his expression, she stopped and reached to touch him.

"The police took him, Leslie. They took him to a jail, in a city in the south. A city named Nakuru."

"Jail, well that's not..." She hesitated. To Firingin, the head of a family going to jail might be one of the worst things that could happen.

Nakuru? she thought. Our tour group stopped at that place. I wouldn't have called it a city.

"Poor Jeiso. He must have been terrified."

"It is said that he fought bravely with his knife."

"Not the one with the missing ruby, I hope."

After the trade of weapons with his grandfather, Firingin had spoken to her about the gem that had been lost from the knife's handle. He'd told her, then, of his long belief that the jewel had been jarred loose when he stabbed the soldier in Maralal. That the police had probably found it. She'd responded, at the time, by telling him not to worry. "The police will not come to a place so remote as this." She'd said that and Firingin had believed her. She'd told him repeatedly in those days that she knew about the police. That every American knew about the police. He'd believed that too.

Firingin touched his own weapon. He rubbed the handle as if feeling for the missing gem.

"If I had not come to his village," he whispered. "If I had refused to trade the knife...."

"If a lot of things. But you forget the joy you gave Jeiso when you brought his caravan back after the accident. He celebrated your return as if you were a conquering hero. And he rejoiced in our marriage, in his hopes for our future. Even now, he looks forward to the birth our child, his first great-grandchild."

"But he is in jail... or maybe dead."

"You don't know that. Perhaps they've just asked him a few questions. Maybe he's already been released."

Firingin's eyes flashed with anger. "You do not know these things. You talk of the police as if you can tell what they will do, but you can not."

She felt the chill of resentment in his voice.

"I will go," he blurted. "I will go to save him."

She gasped and then yelled, "Have you lost your mind? You can't go all the way to Nakuru. It must be a thousand miles from here." It probably wasn't anywhere near that far, but walking, as Firingin would, it might as well be. "Besides, you don't even know where it is."

He stared at her for a long moment. "I will go to the police in South Horr. I will tell them that I am the one who killed the soldier. They will then take me, and they will allow Jeiso to be free."

Terrified, she grabbed for him.

He pulled back.

She tried to calm herself before saying more.

His eyes darted to the doorway.

She spoke in a voice intended to be deliberate and persuasive. "Yes, you can go to the police. We did see some in South Horr when we were there with Hedad, but..."   She would think a moment before she continued. She had to be sure she said the next part the right way.

"It is true, that I do not know all about the police. Especially the police in Kenya. But I do know one thing. If you go to them, I will never see you again...."   Tears choked the words, and she took a breath and waited. Firingin did not speak..

After a time, she continued. "Another thing: you can't be sure that telling the Kenyan police of the stabbing will free Jeiso."

"Why would they keep him after they had me?"

Hoping the question meant he might reconsider, she tried to answered in a convincing way. "Because, my husband, you turning yourself in would show the police a connection between you and Jeiso—a connection they are now only guessing at."

Obviously confused, Firingin shook his head.

She tried again. "At this point the police may not know that you and Jeiso are related. Unless your grandfather has said more than I think he will, the police know nothing for certain."

Firingin continued to look puzzled, and she searched her brain for a more understandable approach.

His eyes hardened with anger. "You do not know if the police know things. You talk too much about what is in the minds of the Kenyans."

He backed away from her and toward the doorway.

She tried to lunge for him, but her body would not respond.

Something in Gof's herbs must have weakened her.

Firingin disappeared from view, and the witch doctor materialized.

"Firingin!" shouted Leslie.

The healer's hands pushed her down to the bedmat.

She turned her head away from the smell and felt her body shiver.

She felt a nudge at her shoulder and looked.

The feathered man leaned toward her, holding up a bowl of his herbal tea.

13

Firingin made ready for the trip back. He repaired frayed places in the lead ropes and spliced broken straps on the load carrier. He would take the she-camel with him as far as Jeiso's village and would return her to Keigo. Keigo would tell Jeiso when the old one came back from the prison.

The angry words Firingin had spoken to Leslie tasted bitter in his mouth. He wanted to tell her that he had meant none of them, that he wished for nothing more than to have the life they'd had before, but he would not. By evening he must be ready to go from this place, and an important thing still needed to be done. He must find the head elder and speak to him of Leslie's care.

With the repair work finished, Firingin led the heifer-camel to the village courtyard. If the headman were there, Firingin would offer the beast to him as a trade.

Once again, the village elder was not to be seen. Firingin asked several men where the leader might be found. One directed him to the dwelling of the headman's number one wife.

A short walk to that place, and Firingin saw the man with the box-hat sitting by the doorway, smoking on a water pipe.

"I will go tonight," announced Firingin.

"Go?"

"I will leave here and surrender myself to the police."

"You cannot. We have spoken of this. Your woman is not ready for such traveling."

"She will not go with me."

The headman's eyes opened wide. "If you surrender, you will not come back to this place. What are we to do with this white woman you would leave with us?"

"It is what I came to talk about. I will trade this young beast to you as payment for the woman's keep."

The headman smiled a tired smile.

"And how long would the woman be here?"

Firingin shook his head. "I do not know. When I go south to save Jeiso, I will stop at his village and tell the one named Keigo where Leslie is. If I do not return, Keigo will send a caravan for her."

The headman's face wrinkled to a frown. "Grandson of Hedaidile, you will not return from the police. When you surrender yourself, they will put you in a cage, and you will see no one. You won't even know if Jeiso is released."

"I will not change my mind," answered Firingin. "But before I leave here, I need to know that my wife has a place for her living."

The headman stared a moment.

"Very well then, do as you wish, but I must have more than an unbroken heifer to keep your woman. Only if you also give the she-camel you brought to our village, will I give your wife a home for as long as she may need one."

Firingin shrank from the proposal. The old camel was not his to trade.

"I cannot give you that beast."

The headman looked hard at Firingin. "I cannot keep the woman unless I have both animals. Your Leslie brings the risk of danger to my village. This we talked about yesterday."

Firingin thought a moment. "I will pay you goods that I have brought for our trip, cooking pots, tools, my tent. I will look through my packs..."

The head elder held up his hands. "Both beasts, or you must stay and work, as you have, to pay for the woman's care. These are my terms."

Firingin thought on the headman's words.... If I do not make the trade, I will be forced to wait, maybe a round moon or two, before Leslie is healed enough for riding the camel.

"You speak a promise?" he asked the headman. "For the two beasts, you will make all the care for Leslie until people come for her?"

"As I have said."

"And you will make care for the child if it is born before she leaves?"

"Most certainly. All children are cared for here."

Firingin knew he would not be allowed to keep the old camel and still go, as he must, to the police. Jeiso would forgive him for trading the animal, that he also knew.

Vowing, if he returned from the Kenyans, to bring another camel for his grandfather, Firingin nodded. "I will take the trade you offer."

The headman smiled.

Firingin backed away to leave, but the headman raised a hand. "You go tonight?"

"After the winds have died."

"And you would go on foot and would carry your food and your water on your back?"

The headman's questions seemed to reveal doubt, and Firingin gave them no further answer.

"South of here, there have been many raids by the Turkana."

"The Turkana will have no interest in me. I will carry nothing of value to them."

"Perhaps not, but I have another way for you to go. I have a salt caravan that needs to go to South Horr. South Horr is a Kenyan town on the way to Nakuru."

The new words brought interest to Firingin.

"The men who work in my corral tell me you have experience

as a driver."

Firingin made no objection.

"For my salt expedition I have need of a driver with experience who also has courage. Your actions have shown that you do not shrink from danger."

Firingin listened.

"Because of the attacks by desert raiders, I have sent few trading ventures into the south this season, but I have Danakil salt in my corral that must be moved before the rains come. The time for rains will be soon, and the salt would wash into the ground if it stayed here."

Firingin felt the hand of manipulation in the elder's lengthy story, but an excitement grew with each word.

"My salt caravan will be guarded from desert bandits by two warriors armed with rifles. The caravan drivers will be boys, those who have no belief in danger. I cannot find men in my village who will risk another passage."

Firingin's mind leapt ahead of the words. "Would your caravan pass near Jeiso's village?"

"Yes, it could stop at that place. I would direct its leader, an elder little older than the boys he would command, to make such a detour. Perhaps he could sell the salt to the Hedaidile clan. If he did so, the trip across the southern desert would not be needed."

Firingin smiled. "I could show your young elder to the man who does the buying."

The headman nodded. "Good. I will tell my leader to make the expedition ready for leaving. He will look for you in the corral after sunset. In the coolness of night, the heavy loading will be done, and before tomorrow morning, the column, and you with it, will start on the trip south."

"And the camels I have traded to you? Who will I give them to?"

"Leave them with those who keep the corral." He paused and stared at Firingin. "I must now tell the warriors who go with the caravan to keep a watch in the sky for police helicopters."

"You fear a police attack on your salt carrier?"

"Perhaps. The Kenyans have ears where no one expects and may find out that you are with the column. If the flying machines circle to land, my warriors will hold you prisoner until the soldiers take you. It is the only way."

Firingin opened his mouth to protest, but the headman gave him a fierce look and continued. "You do not seem a murderer to me, grandson of Hedaidile, but I want no more trouble with the Kenyan police. You may attempt to free Jeiso if you wish; it is your business. But, I have no desire to be discovered as your helper."

Feeling a joy over the bargain struck between him and the village elder, Firingin did not object to the words. Apparently finished with the talking, the head elder settled himself beside his wife's doorway and sought the stem of his water pipe. With good news he wanted to tell Leslie, Firingin hurried to the dwelling of the village healer.

"The woman sleeps," said Gof.

Firingin felt anger. The spirit man uses too many sleeping herbs with Leslie.

"I have come from the headman of this village. Tonight, I leave for South Horr with his salt caravan. I must speak to my woman before I go."

The healer answered with words familiar to Firingin. "She will sleep until tomorrow's sunlight."

Frustration made Firingin want to shout and hit things, but he forced himself to be calm. "When she wakes, you will tell her that I am gone... and that I have made trades of camels for her care. Also, she must hear that I will send people from Jeiso's village for her. Tell her all of those things."

The healer smiled. "As you say, I will tell her."

Firingin looked to the doorway.

"I would look upon her before I go."

Without objection or ceremony, Gof stood aside. Inside, Leslie lay curled on her side as if a sleeping child. The gold velvet of new hair covered top of her head, and her skin had returned to the light color it had been when Firingin first saw her. He touched her. The lashes of her eyes flickered. He waited, but the lashes returned to lie, soft and quiet on her cheeks. He leaned down to place his lips against hers. Her mouth moved to the shape of a smile, but she remained asleep. He felt the moisture of his tears. He wiped them away, and he left.

In the corral, he said goodbye to the old camel and the heifer, then he sat by the fence. How will it be, he wondered, never to see Leslie again... or his child... or Jeiso.

The sun brought the glare of afternoon heat, and Firingin closed his eyes.

Awakened by a rough jolt on his neck and a shout of "Come on, you," he looked up and saw that darkness had come. In front of him stood a man, one younger than himself, but one who spoke with much authority.

"Get up," said the man. "You must help load the beasts and hitch them for leaving."

Firingin stood.

"I am told that you know about caravans," said the young elder. Firingin shrugged. "I was to be a caravan leader at my last village."

"A leader?"

Firingin nodded.

The young man grinned. "You will not be a leader on this trip." He held up a knife—Firingin's knife.

"I took this from you while you slept. You are to be our prisoner. The headman has told me that we will take you to jail when we reach South Horr."

Firingin felt dislike for this smirking elder.

"We are going together to Jeiso Hedaidile's village and maybe on to South Horr, but I will go by myself to the police."

The leader shook his head. "It is true, we will stop at Hedaidile's village, but that man never buys all of our salt. We will go to South Horr, and when we get there, I and my warriors will deliver you to the Kenyans."

Firingin turned to go back to the courtyard. He would find the headman and explain again that he would surrender himself to the police.

He took a step toward the opening in the corral fence and saw that his way was blocked by two rifle-carrying warriors.

"Your guards for the trip," smiled the elder. Firingin might have forced his way past the youthful warriors, but he would not try. Soon they would be companions on the long and hazardous trip, and fighting now would make them enemies from the start. If the caravan goes all the way to South Horr, I will see how much desire these guards or their leader have for going to the police.

He joined the drivers loading the cargo and helped them lever blocks of salt from the stack in the corner of the corral and move the large masses, one by one, to carriers on kneeling camels.

He threw himself into the effort, and several of the boys smiled at him. One or two seemed afraid.

Long after midnight the beasts were loaded. The leader barked commands, and fourteen camels, laden with twenty-four blocks of Danakil salt, and bundles of water, food and other supplies, groaned to their feet. The animals were hitched, nose to tail, and as shadows in the darkness, they plodded their way onto the main trail south of the village.

Walking at his station off the lead camel, Firingin surveyed the entourage.

At the head of the column, the leader strode in all his self-important glory. Firingin's anger faded. A feeling of sympathy had come for the youthful elder. The pride shown now would soon be replaced by the sober look of one who carried too much responsibility.

Behind Firingin marched one of the warriors. Far from being an adult, he would have been a candidate in the most recent of Rendille age sets. He carried a poor rifle and watched his prisoner through narrowed eyes.

The second warrior walked on the far side of the column. He also carried a poor rifle.

The drivers, some of them now singing and some calling in the darkness to their companions, walked at the rear of the caravan.

Firingin thought of the times when he had traveled out with Hedad's expeditions, and he remembered the joy of good comrades and good laughs. He remembered the joys of those days, but he knew that the trip he now started would not be joyous. With heavily loaded camels, it would be hard; with threats of Turkana and police along the way, it would be dangerous; and at the end, it would arrive at a place Firingin feared to go.

Leslie finished her breakfast of millet and some uniden-
tifiable kind of meat. It wasn't bad, but she wouldn't ask the
feathered man for the recipe.

She watched with haunted eyes as her healer performed his rou-
tine of tossing bones and skins on the floor. He finished the inspec-
tion of the objects he'd thrown, and Leslie looked toward the door-
way, half-expecting to see Firingin.

She did not.

She bit her lip, and in a gesture she knew to be futile, she pointed
at the opening. "Firingin, my husband, is he...?"

Gof glared at her. Then he woofed.

A new sound from this man of spirits. Maybe, he would now
metamorphosize into a dog, warning barks and all.

She laughed hysterically then cried, hiding her face in the
bedmat. She'd hoped that soon she'd be away from this sleep cham-
ber, maybe living in the surrounding village and starting the life she
wanted. But Firingin, after popping in and out like a bird on a
cuckoo-clock, was apparently gone. She was stuck here, alone with...

The spirit man touched her arm. She looked at him and saw
the bowl of sleeping potion. She screamed and knocked the vessel
out of his hand, spilling the contents on the floor.

With calm determination, the feathered man picked up the container and poured a refill.

She glared at him and screamed as loud as she could. He glared back and woofed.

Her anger growing, she screamed directly into his face.

The spirit man rocked back on his heels.

She looked away from him and stared at the doorway.

He edged toward her, carefully guarding the bowl.

She took a swipe but missed. He woofed again, menacing. No taming this dog.

The spirit man spoke, his Swahili almost undecipherable, but she managed to make out words for "rest," and "baby."

He knows I'm pregnant! But why does that surprise me? He's a doctor...or supposed to be. He seems concerned. My God! What if I've lost my baby while I've been blacked out in this place!

She lay motionless, trying to assess sensations inside her body.

She still felt pregnant.

She reached down and touched her abdomen. The bulge was still there, a little bigger in fact.

She sought the eyes of the spirit man. Maybe her Swahili would work better than his. "Baby?" she said, pointing to the area below her midriff.

He smiled.

"I still have it?"

He smiled again and then produced another string of mostly unintelligible words.

The word baby again, but this time "lives" in the string.

"Rest, rest," he kept saying, and "baby" and "lives."

He seems to want me to rest so my baby will live.

Again, the feathered one held the bowl toward her. "Mistress rest."

This is impossible. She pointed again at the doorway and once more said Firingin's name.

Another woof. This time accompanied by waving with far-away motions.

No mistaking the meaning. So, Firingin had gone, as he'd threatened—no goodbyes or anything. Like a lemming, he's probably running with his camels, somewhere out in the desert.

Overwhelmed by the thought, she rolled on her side and faced the wall.

Again, the spirit man touched her shoulder, the bowl balanced in his other hand.

She sat and faced him. With blind fury, she pounded on him with her fists.

He took the blows, holding the bowl behind his back. New patterns appeared in the paint on his chest, and still she kept pounding. If he woofed or said anything, she didn't know. The rage in her head had blotted out everything.

In time, exhaustion overcame her, and she fell back on the bedmat.

The spirit man leaned toward her, and with a gentle hand, he lifted her head. He held the potion to her lips.

Sleep would bring escape. She surrendered and drank what he offered.

Through the first night, the train of camels moved south-ward, following, in reverse direction, the path Firingin had taken north with Leslie. At daylight, he started his watch for police flying machines. He watched, but he saw none. If he had, he would have run toward them and surrendered before the caravan's warriors could have made a move to take him.

The column reached the oasis where Firingin and Leslie had stopped, and near the watering hole where he'd tried to cool her fever, it made its first full halt of the expedition. Camels were fed, and one of the boy-drivers prepared a meal of tea and cooked millet.

Firingin helped hobble the beasts then sat and ate his food. One of the two warriors sat beside him. The leader stood nearby.

"Do we move as well as your caravans?" the leader asked Firingin.

Some of the bravado had left the young elder's tone, and Firingin gave him an agreeable answer.

"We moved faster, but our beasts carried lighter loads. We did not carry blocks of salt for trading."

The leader smiled but made no response.

The warrior spoke. "It is said that, in a southern city, you killed a Kenyan soldier."

The question drew the drivers into a circle of listeners. All of the group except the second warrior, who'd been posted to keep watch, pressed close to hear Firingin's answer.

Surprised that his act was known to these boys, he hesitated.

The leader spoke. "Our head elder told us before we left that we were taking you to the Kenyans because you have stabbed one of their officers. We then heard from others that you have killed many..."

Firingin interrupted. "I have killed but one, a Kenyan soldier, but a soldier who had come to kill me with a weapon that shot flaming bullets."

A murmur came from the circle, and the warrior lifted his battered rifle and pointed to it. "It was a weapon such as this one."

Firingin shook his head. "His weapon was the kind that shoots many bullets. The flame from it came as a stream of water into the dark place where I hid. The weapon you hold shoots but one bullet at a time."

The warrior frowned. "I would like to have such a many-bullet-shooting weapon. If I did, the Turkana would fall before me as tent-sticks in a sandstorm."

The leader scowled. "You speak strong words, warrior. You have killed no man—Turkana or any other."

"But I have not a weapon as this man from the south tells about."

"Enough!" said the leader. He then asked Firingin why he had hidden from the soldier. "Kenyans do not search for people without a reason."

Firingin nodded. He would answer to ease the concern of the elder, but he would not embellish the words for the sake of show or entertainment.

"It was in the Kenyan town of Maralal, and the soldiers were there looking for Samburus."

"Samburus?" asked one of the drivers. "Why were soldiers looking for our cattle-herding brethren?"

"A tourist woman was stolen by Samburu warriors. As we have pride in our caravans, the Kenyans have pride in their tourists.

They sent many soldiers to look for the woman and for those who took her."

"But why did they look for you?" asked another driver.

"They looked for all Samburus. I wore Samburu clothing. When the soldier saw me in the darkness he made his weapon shoot bullets into the shadows."

"But you were not hit by them?"

"I had moved and stood behind the soldier."

The driver again: "Why were you hiding there, in the Kenyan town?"

Firingin's patience had grown thin, but he would answer again for these with whom he must travel far. "Elders from the warriors' village said that the tourist woman had to be returned to her people, and they picked me to take her..."

The leader raised a hand to interrupt. "I will now ask the questions." His eyes looked hard into Firingin's face. "You are Rendille, so why were you with the Samburu, and why did their elders ask you to take the tourist woman?"

"I was born among the Samburu. It was after my mother went there as the number one wife to a Samburu man."

"So, you are Samburu then?"

The telling had become complicated, but he must say more. "I am not. Both my father and my mother are Rendille. My mother carried me in her body when she went to be a wife to the Samburu man. He thought me to be his son."

A number of the drivers laughed. All Rendilles, it seemed, enjoyed hearing about tricks played on the Samburu.

The leader waved the boys to silence. "I must ask the questions again." He looked at Firingin. "Why were you picked as the one who would return the woman? And why were you hiding in the Kenyan town?"

Firingin would try once more to explain. "I was picked to take the woman because I know the language of the Kenyans. I was in the town, because I know a schoolmaster there, and would have taken the tourist to him. When I came to his school, the man was not there. I hid in a shed while I waited for his return."

A chorus of questions came from the boy drivers, but the elder walked away, to the lead camel of the caravan. He fumbled in one of the supply bags and removed a small package. The questions stopped, and all watched while he walked back and handed the package to Firingin.

"The passage ahead is dangerous," said the leader. "Your answers have told me that you are a man of honor, not a killer, so I will now give back the knife I took from you in the corral. You may need the weapon if we see bandits."

Without ceremony, Firingin accepted the package. The elder then spoke with authority to the drivers. "We have had enough resting in this place. Go now and prepare the camels for leaving. Do this before Turkana raiders see us standing and talking with our backsides to the desert."

For a moment, Firingin saw a likeness to his cousin Hedad in the new, forthright manner of the young leader.

The caravan crossed the broad wadi south of the oasis and Firingin kept his vigil for police helicopters, but saw only vultures and circling eagles.

Each morning the column stopped for the daily meal and the feeding of camels. Firingin and one of the two warriors always ate near the edge of the group. Firingin learned the names of the warriors, Jaisut, the elder of the two, and Jeiko. The boy-drivers sat and stared from a distance, and no more questions came from them. Firingin did not know the names of the boys. The leader, Karsi, after giving Firingin back the knife also gave his name.

On the morning of the fourth day after leaving the village, the train of camels came to the narrow end of the canyon. The hills had drawn close on both sides and now towered as high and forbidding cliffs.

Karsi called a halt and ordered the two warriors to climb to the ridge-tops. One on each side, the young men would guard the caravan from above.

Drivers and camels stood with the leader and waited for the warriors to reach the assigned stations.

Firingin spoke to Karsi. "You fear an attack in this place?"

The elder nodded toward the opening ahead. "We must now be careful. The passageway narrows, and other caravans have been lost to bandits, the last one was attacked only two round moons ago. Most of its drivers were killed and many beasts with loads of grain were taken."

"A caravan from your village?"

Karsi scanned both ridge-tops before he answered.

"The caravan came from another village, but one of ours passed through the ravine a short time after the attack. They saved several of the wounded, but bodies of dead men, some ripped by the teeth of hyenas, laid among smashed carriers and fallen camels. Five died on that day, one a senior elder of his community."

A look of sadness clouded the young leader's face. "I do not wish to go this way, but I know no other."

"You go here because of a flat passage?" Firingin asked his question, but he already knew the answer. The heavy loads carried by the caravan's camels demanded that the beasts travel over level ground. All other routes out of the valley must pass through steep canyons in the surrounding hills. He and Leslie had descended by one such trail when they came into the basin.

Karsi favored Firingin's question with a nod and again turned his eyes to the ridge-tops.

After a time, came a wave from Jaisut on the left and then from Jeiko on the right.

A gesture from Karsi sent the drivers to their positions, and a whistle from him started the dusty column forward.

On the morning of the third day after Firingin left, Leslie sat on her bedmat and dreamily watched the feathered man go through his routine.

He finished his inspection of the magic trinkets and without saying a word, crawled to the doorway.

She wondered if there might then be a surprise appearance by her husband, but thought otherwise when the healer stopped in the entryway and looked back at her.

Displaying a nearly toothless smile, he beckoned once then crawled outside.

She stared. Am I free to go? She wasn't sure, but she knew she wouldn't reject the possibility. She pushed off the bedmat and scurried like an insect toward the daylight.

Beyond the portal, she squinted in the bright sunlight and beheld her surroundings as a village of some significant size.

Gof sat cross-legged in front of the hut. He motioned to a spot beside him.

In all directions Leslie saw skin-covered dwellings. The same kind as in Jeiso's village. People passed between the huts, but they all seemed afraid to look at her.

She thought of asking Gof why, but decided not to. The subject was far too complicated for the kind of talking she and the healer were able to do. Besides, it probably wasn't her the people were afraid of. More than likely, it was the witch-doctor, himself.

She scanned to spaces beyond the closest dwellings, hoping to get a glimpse of Firingin, but, of course, she saw no sign of him.

In time, Gof seemed to sleep. She wondered if she might walk a little. She stood. The first time she'd put weight on the ankle since the day she jumped off the camel. It felt fine. She took a step, and abruptly, as a stringed puppet, Gof sprang to his feet. He woofed. She laughed then sat down. Behind his painted mask, the spirit man looked amused.

He pointed at the sun. He must think I need a tan. The seven, eight, or however many days she'd spent inside the healer's dwelling had left her more pale than she'd been in months. She pulled back the sleeves of her wrap, turned her face to the incoming rays and wondered if witch-doctors carried suntan lotion. She made a rubbing motion over a reddening place on her right arm.

Gof motioned toward the doorway.

"No, no, I don't want to go inside. Just give me cream for the burning."

He looked puzzled.

"Butter," she said.

He smiled and nodded. A string of words from him brought a woman cringing from the shadows. He spoke a command, and the woman hurried away, returning in minutes with a bowl of brownish paste.

Gof took the bowl and waved the woman away.

In Swahili, Leslie expressed thanks to her but perceived no sign of a reaction.

Bringing a look of horror to Gof's eyes but no verbal objection, Leslie rubbed the paste over her arms and neck, then carefully covered some parts of her face. Without knowing what the concoction contained, she wouldn't apply it near her eyes or mouth. And she wouldn't put any on her head. Though shaved smooth the day before she and Firingin left Jeiso's village, it was now matted all over with downy, blond hair.

She smiled when she thought of the spectacle she and her seated companion must present: him covered with paint and feathers and her alongside him, pink and wearing a crown of peach fuzz.

No wonder people didn't want to look at them.

After what must have been an hour, the same, silent woman brought food: tea, cooked millet, and bits of meat—the same kind of meat that Gof had served inside the hut.

They ate—the woman with them. Then Gof spoke again to her. She left and presently returned with a man walking at her side.

Tall, handsome and middle-aged looking, the man wore an unusually white loin wrap, and a box-shaped hat.

He sat down beside Leslie.

"Hello," he said in English, "I am Jeidid, the head elder of this village."

"You speak English!"

"Adequately, perhaps. I have learned to speak your language in the school at Marsabit."

Finally, someone she could understand.

"So you're the one who talked to my husband."

Jeidid nodded. "I have conversed with that man, of course. But he has gone away to the south."

"To the police."

"Yes, so he said it to me."

Jeidid spoke in Rendille to Gof, and the feathered man stood and retreated with the woman to another hut.

Jeidid spoke again to Leslie, "Your man, Firingin Hedaidile came to me. He traded his camels for your good care here. He said he would tell people in Jeiso Hedaidile's community to come for you."

"He's going to Jeiso's village? Why? The police aren't at Jeiso's village, are they?"

Jeidid shook his head.

"Did he tell you why he went there alone, without me?"

"You could not go with him. You are not yet ready for such travel. But he is not going by himself. He is a driver with one of our caravans. It will stop at the village of Hedaidile on its way to South Horr."

She bit her lower lip and stared at the sky.

The man sat silent.

"Why couldn't he have just waited?" she asked, more to herself than to the elder.

"He worried much about you," replied Jeidid, "and he gave up much for your well-being—both of his camels."

"But still, he left without me."

Jeidid nodded.

"How long before somebody comes?"

Jeidid shrugged. "Maybe weeks or even months. I cannot say."

"And you will keep me here for all that time?"

"It is what I agreed to do. You and perhaps your child, Jeiso Hedaidile's great-grandson I believe."

She shuddered at the thought of being alone and giving birth without her husband, or any person she knew.

Jeidid continued to talk. "Gof says your injury was great, but he has cured you, and now your child will be born healthy."

"So everything's okay?"

"Gof is, of course, not a midwife, but he speaks of your recovery with great joy."

Not a midwife? A feeling of remorse welled up in Leslie as she thought of the wonderful midwife she'd left in Jeiso's village. She felt tears come.

"Do not weep," said Jeidid. "Your husband left here for the best reasons. for his grandfather but also for the Rendille people."

She nodded. "He told me about the attack here. I'm really sorry about that."

"It is behind us now. After Firingin surrenders, the Kenyans will not come again. He knows that and knows also that your child would have lived in shame if he, the child's father, had not sacrificed to end the sufferings."

She stared in disbelief at the man. "He said all that to you?"

"Not all, but I could see the sadness in his eyes. And I could also see that he was sad about leaving you. Gof said that he came to speak to you on the last day, but you were asleep."

"He came to say goodbye?"

"This is true. He looked upon you but could not say the words he wanted to say."

"He could have waited. One day wouldn't have..."

Jeidid interrupted. "The caravan was leaving. He wanted to be with it."

"All for some precious, manly honor."

Jeidid stared for a long moment. "This is true. Firingin wants honor, as I have said, for himself and for his child. Is it not the same in the world you come from? Don't men there sacrifice for honor?"

"I guess they do... some of them... in wars and other things. But think of the suffering wars cause."

Jeidid stood and stretched. "Please, dear woman, I cannot think on suffering of others so far away. The hour grows late, and I must show you to the dwelling where you will live with us."

"By myself, no doubt."

"You will stay with my number-three wife, Deelia. A woman of your age, I believe, and she also speaks a small amount of English."

"Sounds wonderful, but I hope I won't be too much trouble for her."

Jeidid smiled and with one strong hand, lifted Leslie to her feet. She walked beside him, with only slight pain in her ankle, until they came to a dwelling near the center of the complex.

They stopped at the hut's entrance, and Jeidid spoke in Rendille to the person inside. A cheerful sounding voice responded.

"You may enter," Jeidid said to Leslie.

She crawled into the opening. Jeidid followed. The interior of the hut looked the same as those in Jeiso's village: low and dark with a rock fireplace in the middle. Bedding and clothes laid, piled in the back; pots and other utensils, along with containers for food, clustered near the center; a stack of firewood crowded one side of the doorway.

Jeidid made the introductions, speaking in English to Leslie but continuing in Rendille to the woman named Deelia.

The young woman seated by the fireplace smiled and bowed from the waist. "Pleased to meet you," she said. "You are from America! I wish so much I could see that country. I want to look upon buildings that scrape on the sky and have light at night as in the daytime."

Jeidid rumbled a few words in Rendille and left.

Deelia couldn't have been more beautiful. Though not as tall as many Rendille women, she had a figure that was shapely and supple looking; her teeth were straight and even, and her eyes danced with a youthful sparkle. Except for her native costume, and her shaved head, she could have stepped directly from a page in an American fashion magazine.

Lighting a candle, she motioned for Leslie to sit beside her. She poured a bowl of tea and continued talking. "I have never been to any city. Not even Loiyangalani..."

"Loiyangalani? Where is that?"

"Loiyangalani is a trading center to west of here. It is by the lake called Turkana. I have been told these things, but I do not go there."

Leslie sat, silent, wondering why a woman who spoke English with such fluency had never traveled, and why she'd been addressed in Rendille by her English speaking husband. Without warning, Deelia reached out and touched Leslie's fuzzy hair. "It is soft... and so yellow in its color."

Leslie smiled. "My head's usually shaved like yours... or at least it had been for a while. The hair started to grow out again while I was in the healing man's..."

Deelia laughed. "My husband has told me that Gof kept you inside his dwelling while he made you well."

"Yes, made me well. I guess he did that... with herbs and..."

"We live quite remote here. We have no doctors as you have in America. In Marsabit there is a clinic, but Gof is the only kind of healer in this village."

Leslie nodded and asked where Deelia had learned to speak such good English.

Deelia beamed. "Thank you for the compliment, Less lee..." Deelia's competence with the language had not prevented the usual trouble with Leslie's name. "...I have received excellent instruction at the Kenyan school in Marsabit. It is where I met my husband, Jeidid. He is the man who brought you here."

"You were in school together?"

"We loved each other at the Marsabit School, but we were not married then."

"He said that you're his number-three-wife."

"I am as he says, number three." Deelia flashed a proud smile. "He is a most handsome husband, do you not agree."

Leslie nodded. "A nice-looking man."

"I cannot wait until he comes to..." Deelia's eyes showed a hint of shyness. "How is it said in America? ...sleep with me?"

"That's the way it's said." Girl-talk already.

"Would it be impolite of me to ask how often that is? Him coming to you. With three wives and all."

Deelia smiled. "It is not impolite, I think. But Jeidid has four wives, not three, and the older ones have the priority. I am not his newest, but still I have to wait. Usually for a week after he has returned to the village." She paused and looked to the doorway. "But sometimes when he comes, I am not ready for him... It is called period, I think."

Leslie nodded. "Yes, that's what it's called. But if Jeidid met you while you were both in school, why aren't you his first wife?"

"You do not understand the ways of our people. Jeidid had obligations when he returned to this village. His father had selected wives from here for him."

"And, you're not from here?"

"My home village is to the south and east. A small village, much smaller than this one. After my school, I returned there, and I helped my mother."

"Carrying wood and water, I suppose."

Deelia nodded.

"That seems a shame with the knowledge you must have had. And, as attractive as you are."

"Attractive? It is a word I do not know."

"Good-looking...sexy."

Deelia put her hands beside her face and cocked her head with a smile. "You like to look at me, yes?"

"Yes, you're nice to look at. Doesn't Jeidid tell you that?"

"Since we are married, we do not speak of such things, but in school, he looked often on me. He looked, and he found much sex with me."

"I see. Well, I'd say he took a great risk when he let you return, alone, to your mother's village."

Deelia looked puzzled.

"I mean with other young men there. Weren't they interested in you?"

Deelia smiled. "There were men, but they were all poor. My father placed value on me. He asked payment of eight camels. He would have taken cattle, so he talked to a Samburu. It was lucky I was not sold to that man."

"I'm told that's what happened to Firingin's mother. She was sold to a Samburu."

"Firingin?" Deelia's eyes widened. Then she smiled. "Firingin. It is your husband's name?"

"Yes, Firingin is my husband. Not that he's been acting like much of a husband, lately."

An awkward silence, then Deelia continued with her favorite topic.

"Jeidid is a most respected headman among the Rendille people. He was honored by the leaders when they made him, as a young man, the head elder of this village. It is an important village because it guards the slopes of Mount Kulal."

Leslie had deduced earlier that Mount Kulal was the prominent peak in the west.

"Kulal has the best grazing in the region," added Deelia. "Clans, from all over, petition for the right to bring their animals to its high pastures. Jeidid is the one who makes decisions on who receives those privileges and who does not."

"So, he's the big cheese around here."

The slang confused Deelia for a moment, but she didn't let it stop her. "He is big, of course, but he is not the Jesus."

Leslie almost laughed. She considered correcting her hostess, but decided against it. Why add American slang to the woman's already overflowing vocabulary?

Days passed, and Leslie began to yearn for a break in Deelia's constant stream of English. Talking in Leslie's native tongue seemed to be all the young woman wanted to do, and Leslie, with some weakness remaining in her legs and an occasional spotting of blood on her garment, felt she had little choice but to sit and endure the avalanche.

Eventually, after all the pet topics had been covered several times, Deelia's monologue became background noise, and Leslie began to think on her own situation, and what she might do about it. Her anger toward Firingin had cooled, and she wondered if, in time, she might find a way to visit him in jail. Perhaps, after she got back to Jeiso's village, someone would take her. She wondered about the Kenyan system of justice. Would Firingin even be in jail? Maybe the death penalty was automatic for somebody who had killed a... Overwhelmed by the thought, she moaned to herself.

Deelia kept talking.

Leslie thoughts continued: They will probably have a trial for him... Maybe if I went to the police, I could testify on his behalf... tell them that he was trying to return me when the soldier attacked. She wondered if she might get Jeidid to take her to the police.

"Deelia! I need to talk to your husband."

The question interrupted the stream of words, and the young woman's eyes brighten with fear.

"No, don't be afraid. I just need to ask him something."

"Jeidid is not in the village. He is, today, on the mountain with the herders."

"You know when he'll be back?"

Deelia shrugged, and for the first time since Leslie had been with her, she said nothing.

Leslie usually slept late, but one morning, maybe a week after coming to Deelia's place, she awakened to shouting as her hostess returned from chores.

"Leslie! I have something I can now tell you."

"Oh boy." Leslie yawned and rubbed her eyes.

"I can, today, speak about the police raid on our village. Jeidid has said, in the courtyard, that the danger of another attack is over, and people may talk of the first one."

Interested, Leslie sat up in the bed.

"That's strange."

Deelia ignored the comment and picked up on her new monologue. "On that day, I saw the helicopters coming when I returned to my dwelling from the well. In a fleet of three, making a chopping sound, they came low from the south...."

The description brought horrifying memories, but Leslie would not—could not—interrupt the river of Deelia's words.

"...I had seen flying machines at Marsabit, so I knew what they were, but many people in this village did not have my knowledge. The noise made women and children run and scream. Some tried to hide in their dwellings, some in the corral. Men drew knives, and warriors stood with spears raised, a few with rifles. When the soldiers came from their machines with weapons pointed, Jeidid told the men to put away their knives and to lay down their spears and rifles. He knew the power of the Kenyan's weapons. The soldiers moved with great speed, frightening people and tearing holes in dwellings."

When Deelia stopped to take a breath, Leslie interjected, "Firingin told me about the attack, and I'm so sorry..."

Paying no attention, Deelia resumed. "Men of the village were taken to the courtyard, and there they were made to wait while the officer in charge asked questions. He spoke in English, and only

Jeidid could answer... I tried, from the edge of the opening, to listen, but Jeidid saw me and told me to go away."

"So you didn't hear what was said?"

"I did hear some of the officer's words, from the place where I hid. I heard him ask about a man from Hedaidile's village and a white woman.... I heard him ask about you and your husband."

Leslie looked away. "So everyone here knows about Firingin and me?"

"Not everyone. Nobody except Gof could speak to you, and only Gof and one elder at the corral could speak to your husband. It is the way Jeidid wanted it. He risked trouble when he brought you into the village and hoped the people would not find out that you and your husband were the ones the police looked for."

"But why did he take such a risk? Why didn't he just send us on our way? I probably wouldn't have survived, but..."

A look of astonishment came over Deelia's face. "Jeidid would never send you to die in the desert! He would care for any Rendille in trouble. Your husband is a member of the Hedaidile family. Jeidid would have lost much respect among the Rendilles if he had turned away the grandson of Jeiso Hedaidile."

"But what if the police come back? Jeidid has put his village in great danger, hasn't he?"

Deelia's somber look turned to a smile. "Jeidid is a great leader. He understands such things as danger, but now the danger is over. Your husband has gone to surrender to the Kenyans. Jeidid has said in the courtyard that the police will not come again."

Leslie wondered how such a great leader could be so niave. Under police questioning, Firingin would probably be forced to tell where she could be found, and, no doubt, they would soon come for her...

"I need to find Jeidid", she said to Deelia.

"Herdsmen from another place talk to him today. I know this because he told me that he would be busy until tonight when he will come to see me."

"He will be here tonight?"

"Yes, but it will not be for talking."

"Oh. Well, maybe I can talk to him tomorrow."

"Why do you need to talk to Jeidid?"

Leslie smiled. "It's just something I forgot to tell him, before."

"Something you cannot tell me."

Leslie smiled again. "Not now, I can't."

Deelia shrugged. Then she rummaged near the fireplace and found a scissors and a razor blade. "Let us sit outside," she said. "I will shave your head. It is best that you do not have so much hair to keep clean."

Leslie willingly sat by the doorway, and Deelia, snipped away the yellow fuzz and shaved the bristles down to the skin. Leslie sensing that Deelia brooded, tried to think of a way to bring a smile to her face.

"Deelia, tell me something in the English you speak so well."

Deelia looked at her with suspicious eyes.

Leslie tried again. "Have you ever thought of teaching some of your language skills to children in this village? ...in a school, I mean."

Deelia shook her head. "A school for speaking English? Why?"

"It's an important language in Kenya. In Nairobi, people in shops, and hotels, all speak English... other places too. The boys and girls of this village would be able to get good jobs..."

Deelia looked puzzled. "But the Kenyans have the school in Marsabit."

"And all the children of this village go there?"

"No, children must live at that school. Only those who are from rich families or have relatives near Marsabit can go. I lived there with my eldest sister."

Leslie smiled. "See, that's what I mean. A school here could be used to teach those who cannot go to Marsabit. I taught the children of Hedaidile's village, and everyone there thought it was great."

Deelia looked worried. "Did they learn the English from you?"

"English? Yes, a little, but I taught reading and numbers too."

"But English is what makes me special for Jeidid."

"Oh, I doubt if that's all that makes you special."

"I would not want everyone to have words to speak in his language."

Leslie thought a moment. "But, don't you think Jeidid might be proud to have a village where the children all talked in English... knew numbers and..."

Deelia looked away.

After the evening meal, as advertised, Jeidid arrived. Deelia asked Leslie to wait outside, and, respecting the conjugal visit, Leslie made a hurried exit, settling herself a distance from the doorway. Hoping she wouldn't be on an all night vigil, she looked up at the stars and tried not to hear the sounds inside.

In no more than fifteen minutes, Jeidid emerged. He saw her and looked a moment, but she did not speak to him. His time inside had been so short it seemed almost certain that he and Deelia weren't finished. He'll go back to her, she thought, but Jeidid did not go back to Deelia. He left, walking toward the village court-yard. Leslie struggled to her feet and would have followed him, but Deelia came out and stood, smiling, her face seeming to glow in the moonlight. "Oh Leslie, he is so strong. He comes to me and his body is so hard. Already, I miss the feel of him."

Leslie said nothing. To her, it seemed a tragedy that this beautiful person expected so little from her husband.

"Tonight I was ready for him," said Deelia. "Soon I will have his first child, I think."

"First child? With four wives, he hasn't any children?"

"It is so. None of us has been able to bring our husband an heir. It is a great shame to all in this village that their leader has been so badly served by his wives."

"You think it's your fault, you and the other wives?"

"Most certainly. Jeidid is strong and powerful. He has the seed of many children in his body."

Leslie shook her head and said nothing.

Inside the canyon, all the drivers became silent. Their usual chatter ceased, and nothing could be heard but the creak of carriers and the occasional grunt of a camel.

About half an hour into the passage, the column filed into a sharp turn, and presently, high walls obscured the animals and drivers behind from those in front.

Firingin expected Karsi to urge the train to move faster, but the young leader continued for several slow steps, then stopped altogether. The lead camel and those behind came to a halt, and the column stood, pinched around the hard corner, with six of its fourteen animals still behind the turn.

Shouts came from the stranded boys, but Karsi stood, staring at the ridge-tops ahead. Firingin looked and saw nothing unexpected, then a scream came from the high ground on the right. He took a step to get a better view and still saw nothing. Another scream, then a pleading sound followed by a truncated wail.

Firingin looked for a place where the caravan might take cover and saw an outcropping at the side of the canyon, a shelter for hiding, perhaps a barricade from which to fight.

He motioned to the boys he could see and to the leader.

Two drivers came running, but Karsi stood, frozen in front of the camels.

Firingin led the boys along a shale surface by the canyon wall. They reached the outcropping and found a shallow depression in the rock, a place too small for the camels and their loads but big enough for the drivers. Firingin waved the two inside and then drew his knife.

He leaned around the edge of the outcropping and surveyed the scene. The boys crouched behind him. He could feel their fast breathing against his back.

A few beasts in the visible part of the column flicked their ears, and one bellowed, but none moved, neither forward nor back. Karsi stood with mouth open, his feet planted on the canyon floor.

The sounds from above had stopped. Firingin told the boys to wait, and he stepped from behind the rocks. He might yet have time to bring the leader and perhaps other drivers.

A chanting and a whooping came from ahead in the canyon. Firingin saw Karsi look toward the sounds and watched a mask of horror moved across the young face.

The chanters marched into view, and Firingin moved back to the outcropping. One of the marchers wore the traditional white feathers of a Turkana warrior, and behind him, came four others, two holding a spear between them. Atop the spear rode the bloody gourd of a severed head! A gasp came from one of the boy drivers. Though smeared with red and bits of gristle, the head was clearly recognizable as that of the warrior from the right hilltop, Jeiko, the one who had wished for the fire-spitting rifle.

A single shot from a weapon carried by one of the quartet behind the feathered Turkana, and Karsi dropped to his knees.

Several of the camels bolted.

Ignoring the man they'd just shot, the Turkana planted the spear holding their bloody trophy and all but the feathered one ran to capture camels. Firingin crowded the boys back to the hiding place and took a position at the edge of the rocks. He leaned forward and saw the feathered Turkana shouting directions to others. In time, the four raiders returned with three nervous-looking camels in tow.

The feathered bandit took the animals, and the other Turkana resumed their chant and started jumping and dancing around their grisly standard. The feathered warrior stood by the lead camel and placed a foot on Karsi's neck.

After a drumming round of cheers and a series of vertical leaps, all Turkana warriors except the feathered leader filed toward the rear of the caravan, and soon screams and wails came from beyond the rocks.

The feathered warrior hobbled the lead camel and hooked the others in a line behind her. He checked cargo on some of carriers, then, almost as an afterthought, he drew his knife and leaned over the caravan leader.

Firingin knew, that instant, that he could not stand idly by and watch the bloody rendering of another trophy. He ran at full speed from the outcropping and toward the Turkana.

The villain, so occupied with the treachery he intended, did not look up, and without a shout or a warning, Firingin leaped the final distance and sank the blade of Jeiso's old knife into the back of the feathered bandit's neck. The Turkana died without a sound.

Watching toward murderous cries still coming from beyond the turn in the canyon, Firingin dragged the inert form of Karsi to a thicket of thorn bushes.

A shot rang out from the left ridge. The warrior, Jaisut must have found his courage. Sounds of shooting came from ground level. The lead camel broke her hobble and ran. The other beasts followed her, some tearing their ties and loping for separate freedoms. Straps holding several carriers ripped loose. Blocks of salt shattered on the ground.

Firingin crouched behind the thorn bushes and watched. He would not drag Karsi into the open until he knew the attackers were gone.

Presently, the four Turkana warriors came from behind the bend and dispersed in the direction of the lose camels. One stopped a moment and regarded his feathered comrade's body then hurried on.

Karsi laying at Firingin's feet, moaned. Though blood oozed from his left shoulder, the leader was alive. He spoke, but his words made no sense. Firingin placed a hand over Karsi's mouth and commanded silence.

Flies swarmed to the dark mass crusting on the leader's shoulder. Firingin, with eyes focused in the direction of the Turkana, paid no attention to the insects.

He noticed a flock of vultures landing near the body of the feathered warrior, and a pair of hyenas sniffing from the other side of the canyon. Soon, those scavengers would be fighting over the feast he had laid before them. He would try to ignore the dismemberment.

One of the raiders came into view leading a captured camel. A shot rang out from the ridge—Jaisut still kept a watch. Two more Turkana came running, and they all took cover under a rocky overhang.

Silence from above while the Turkana hid, but in time, they crept back into the open. Another shot greeted them, and dust rose near one of the bandits. The others ran, but the one nearly hit knelt and fired his weapon.

A quick discharge from the ridge, and the raider fell and lay screaming and thrashing on the canyon floor.

A fourth shot, and the screaming stopped.

One of the remaining Turkana ventured forth. He looked at his fallen comrade, but another shot came, and the bandit ran.

Presently Firingin saw the three Turkana warriors walking with four captured camels. Looking toward the top of the left wall, the raiders filed northward, slinking behind the bodies of the camels.

The procession moved past the thicket where Firingin hid and also past the Turkanas' dead companions. Soon the bandits were gone, obscured by the bend in the canyon wall.

Firingin stayed hidden. He'd heard stories of Turkana leaving the scenes of their treachery only to return and surprise the unwary.

The vultures flew back to the carrion. Hyenas moved in from the shadows.

Firingin tried to give water to Karsi, but the leader would not open his lips. Coolness of shade would be needed to revive him.

A red clad figure moved across the valley floor.

Perhaps thinking himself the only survivor, Jaisut had come down from his perch. He stopped and looked at the bloody head of Jeiko, then sat by the far wall of the canyon and cried.

Firingin stepped from behind the thicket and waved his arms. The young warrior stood and immediately pointed his weapon. With haste, Firingin spoke. "Jaisut, do not shoot. I am Hedaidile from the caravan."

Jaisut lowered his rifle and walked forward. Firingin would attempt to keep the young man's attention away from the gory relic of their murdered comrade. He smiled and gestured toward the body of the Turkana who'd been shot.

"You fire your weapon well."

A self-conscious grin from Jaisut. "I learned shooting from the headman of our village. He learned from Kenyans at his school. They wanted him to be a soldier, I think."

Firingin raised a hand. "Two drivers hide behind the rocks, but Karsi is here, in this thicket, laying as one who is dead." Jaisut's face showed fear.

"No, come," said Firingin. "He will live, I believe. But he needs the coolness of shade."

The warrior turned to leave. "I will catch the beasts left by the Turkana."

Knowing that he could not move the leader alone without risking additional injury, Firingin spoke with authority. "You will stay, and later we will send the drivers to catch the beasts."

The tone in Firingin's voice caused Jaisut to wait.

"I need you to help me carry the leader to shelter."

Jaisut nodded, and with reluctance, he followed Firingin to the place where Karsi lay under the bushes. With eyes closed, he then helped Firingin move the broken body away from the thicket.

The boy-drivers showed great fear when they saw their leader coming as limp cargo, and not wanting to deal with more frightened helpers, Firingin ordered them to capture the camels.

The boys left, and Firingin spoke to Jaisut. "We must make haste. The Turkana will soon come back to this place."

Jaisut shook his head. "Those attackers will not return. They are now running north across the desert. From above, I watched them go."

"You should have shot more when you saw them going."

Jaisut shrugged and opened the breach of his rifle. The metal of the chamber gleamed empty. Firingin nodded and turned his attention to the leader. He took the water gourd from Karsi's waist-belt and placed the vessel to the parched lips. He poured, but the liquid ran down both sides of Karsi's face. The young elder coughed and opened his eyes.

Jaisut took several steps backward but didn't run.

"You have been shot by the Turkana," said Firingin to Karsi.

Karsi moaned, but said nothing.

Firingin examined the wound and saw that the bullet had gone in close to the base of the neck but had not stayed within the body.

"Wak is with you," said Firingin.

Karsi did not respond.

Firingin asked a question. "Why did you stand in the canyon when I motioned? Why did you not come away and hide with me and the boys?"

Without answering, Karsi closed his eyes.

The warrior spoke. "Perhaps he saw the flash of Turkana feathers on the ridge above and knew he could not hide."

Firingin nodded and looked back to the leader. From the elder's loin wrap, Firingin tore a piece of cloth and dampened it with water. He washed away the dried blood, and when the new bleeding stopped, he poured water where clay had collected near the wall.

"Mix this to mud," he told Jaisut. "Then make a plaster and use it to cover his wound."

While Jaisut worked, Firingin walked to the edge of the out-cropping and looked for the boy-drivers. No sight of them. Only whoops and yelling from the canyon.

"I will now go and help with the beasts. You stay and give water to Karsi when he wakes."

Jaisut held up a hand. "One of us must bury the drivers who were killed."

Firingin winced. In his concern for the leader, he'd forgotten the boys behind the bend.

"They were all killed," added Jaisut. "I saw it from above. The Turkana stabbed them then shot the ones who did not die. A beast was also shot when a Turkana's shooting of a driver missed."

Firingin stretched his body tall. "I will see to it."

From the site of the killings, a swarm of vultures lifted as a gray carpet from the canyon floor. Three hyenas and one jackal gorged on the remains of the dead camel. Firingin yelled, and the wild creatures retreated a distance. He pulled a shovel from the pack of the dead camel and dug a single pit for the bodies of the drivers and for the pieces of severed limbs.

He gathered rocks from the area and piled them over the grave, then he captured the two camels that grazed on grass in the canyon's shadow.

Back at the outcropping, he found Jaisut sitting with eyes fixed on the leader.

Firingin greeted the warrior, and looking embarrassed, the young man jumped to his feet. "You have already finished?"

Firingin nodded. "I brought back two beasts that I found on the other side. They are hobbled outside. Both have blocks of salt on their backs."

Jaisut said nothing.

"Have the drivers I sent to the canyon returned?"

The warrior shook his head.

"Perhaps they are still fearful of looking upon Karsi. I will go and see if they have caught any of the beasts."

Jaisut looked hard at Firingin. "Why is it you do these things? You know I have no shooting bullets in my weapon. Why do you not escape from us?"

Firingin shook his head. "I have no wish to escape, to run and to live my life in hiding."

Jaisut smiled a weak smile but made no reply.

"If we get away from here, we can go to the village of my grandfather, Jeiso Hedaidile. There, we will find those who will give us shelter and will care for our wounded comrade."

"But I do not know the way to Hedaidile's village."

"No matter, I will show you how to go. The way leads opposite to the one I traveled north with my woman."

Jaisut looked apprehensive.

"Do not be fearful. If we leave here soon, we will be in the desert before the Turkana return, and they will not attack in the open. Your shooting has frightened them, and they do not know that your weapon is empty. Three days, maybe four, and we will be in the village, and you will be safe."

The warrior's lips moved toward a smile, and he nodded.

"Now, I must go search for the boy drivers, and you must keep the watch over Karsi."

A short distance from the outcropping, Firingin saw the caravan's lead camel, a beast that seemed to have a calm disposition. He clucked as he approached the creature, and the animal picked up its ears. Continuing the soothing sounds, he walked close and grabbed the lead rope. He stroked the animal's face and led her toward the latest hoot he'd heard from the boys. Presently, he saw one of the young drivers chasing a panicked camel toward the far wall of the ravine.

"Stop," Firingin shouted. "You cannot catch a beast by running at it."

The boy halted and looked at Firingin. The frightened camel shuffled to a walk and then stood. With a heavy load still on its back, it could have been grateful for a chance to rest.

Firingin motioned for the boy to come, but the boy did not move.

"Why do you stay away?" said Firingin.

The young one's eyes opened wide, but he said nothing. Firingin took a step forward. The driver turned and ran.

"Stop!" yelled Firingin. The boy stopped.

"Why do you run?"

"I fear you. I saw you, with your knife, run and stab the Turkana."

Firingin shook his head. He did not want to be feared. "The feathered warrior would have cut our leader's body apart. I could not..." The boy ran again. Firingin let him go. He clucked to the standing camel and held out his hand. In a short time, he caught the creature and then led a parade of two beasts down the canyon. He again saw the young driver who ran. The other boy came also, leading a captured camel.

Firingin motioned to the second driver. "Come forward with your beast, and we will tie it to our new caravan."

The boy approached, smiling the smile of admiration. He stood a distance away while Firingin linked the camel to the train. Firingin smiled at the boy. He must attempt to be a leader for these young ones. "Your name?"

The boy stared, not answering.

"How is it you are called?" said Firingin.

"Hedad," said the boy.

Surprised to hear the same name as his lost cousin, Firingin repeated it. "Hedad?"

The boy nodded. "Hedad Maikonbile."

Firingin tried a smile. "Hedad, I do not wish you and your companion to fear me. I have killed but two times. I did not want it, not the first time, and not the second time."

The boy's eyes glowed with admiration. "You must be a great warrior in the village of your family."

The other boy approached, listening to hear Firingin's response.

Firingin hesitated. Then he spoke carefully.

"I am one who cares for animals, cattle and camels. I have never been a warrior."

The boys looked puzzled. Hedad, the braver of the two, spoke. "Then you must be a man of spirits. No other can become an elder without first being a warrior. You..."

"Enough!" shouted Firingin. He looked toward the bend in the canyon.

"I cannot speak more of this. The Turkana will soon return from the desert, and we must be gone before they come. Go now, and capture beasts. Go and make clucks to calm them. Then walk, slow, and when you have your hands on them, bring the animals here to join the others."

Shadows of late afternoon stretched across the canyon floor, but only six camels had been retrieved. No others could be found. Firingin and the boys took the train of animals, only four loaded with cargo, to a place beside the outcropping.

Behind the rocks, Jaisut waited. Firingin pointed to the sleeping leader. "Has he awakened?"

"His eyes have opened, but they closed again. I fear he cannot walk from here."

"We will carry him," said Firingin.

"But he will make a heavy load."

"We cannot leave him, to be found by the Turkana or eaten by the hyenas. We must carry him. I will start and..." He turned and looked at the boy who stood in the shadows. "...and you will help me."

Terror filled the boy's eyes. He started to cringe backwards.

"Stay!" said Firingin. He would use his fierce reputation to make these young ones do what they must.

"What is your name?"

The boy gulped.

The warrior spoke. "Kaido. His name is Kaido. He is my half-brother. We are from the family of Wambile."

The warrior pointed to the fallen leader. "That one is my cousin. He is also Wambile. It is a large family."

Firingin held up a hand. "Stop. We cannot stand here, naming names. Darkness comes, and we must be gone from here."

The boy named Kaido laughed a nervous laugh, stopping when

Firingin stared at him.

Jaisut, still caught up in the process he had started, said, "And you are Firingin. It is a Samburu name, but you are not Samburu. You are..."

The boy Kaido choked back another laugh, and Firingin felt embarrassment. He said to the boy, "Go and bring a tent and four poles from the lead camel's pack. We will make a mat for bearing the leader."

The boy left and Firingin spoke to Jaisut. "You must also go. You must make the caravan ready. Until we pass from this canyon, you will lead the beasts."

A new look of anxiety came to Jaisut's eyes. "I cannot. I have told you this. The way from this place is not known to me."

Pointing in the direction of travel, Firingin spoke in a strong voice. "We will go between the canyon walls as we were going before the attack."

"But there will be places where the path goes in two directions."

With his patience failing, Firingin tried to keep calm as he spoke. "Yes, this is true, and those will be places where we must decide which path to follow. When we come to such places, I will help you."

With obvious reluctance, Jaisut nodded and moved toward the entrance where he was met by the boy Hedad who carried an armload of materials.

Out of breath, Hedad spoke. "Kaido stays with the beasts. I will help with the carrying." Jaisut appeared angry. "The carrying was to be Kaido's task. Why is it you come in his place?"

Hedad beamed at Firingin. "Kaido says he fears walking with this one. But I do not fear."

Jaisut's eyes sought Firingin's. "I will bring my half-brother."

Firingin, looked to the sky. Never before had he seen a caravan so much in need of a leader. "No, we must not use time for such. Hedad wants to help with the building of the carrier and with the carrying, so I will let him. You must now go, and with Kaido, you must make ready for the leaving."

Jaisut stalked from the shelter.

Firingin nodded to Hedad. "You spread the tent cloth for the mat. I will tie on the poles."

After the morning chores, Deelia, in a state of happy reverie, started looking through her stock of sewing goods. "My baby will want a pretty wrap, don't you think?" she said to Leslie.

Leslie nodded to the question then excused herself. Rather than listen to Deelia prattle about a baby that probably wouldn't be born, she would make an early trip to the courtyard and look for Jeidid.

Along the way she met several women. She smiled but received no recognition from them. At the central plaza, she saw only men. They stood in groups, talking, or squatted, playing board games. Jeidid was not among them.

Leslie sat in the shade of a hut that faced the open area. She sat and waited for two hours, maybe more, and she did not see the village elder. The heat grew intense and she had to give up her vigil. Hoping that Deelia would, by now, be quietly stitching baby clothes, she returned to the dwelling.

The walk had not been far, and she'd sat all the while she'd waited, but still she felt almost faint with fatigue. She thought it might be the heat, but the weak feeling remained through the rest of the day. She worried but said nothing until the following morning when she saw several spots of blood on her bedding.

She showed the spots to Deelia. "I think you'd better bring Gof or somebody."

Deelia's eyes brightened, horrified. "I will ask Ulana. She is the best midwife in our village."

Leslie had no reason to object, and that afternoon a sturdy looking woman came. She entered the dwelling without social formalities and spoke in an almost manly voice. The voice rasped an undecipherable dialect, and Leslie asked Deelia to interpret.

"Ulana wants you to remove your wrap," said Deelia.

Leslie complied and the next words from Ulana translated to: "You are not Rendille. I have never, before, worked with one of your kind."

Leslie almost laughed. "The equipment is the same, isn't it?"

Deelia did not to pick up on the humor. She spoke solemnly to the midwife.

The response: "Ulana has been midwife for many births. She understands such things."

Leslie smiled, but inside she felt the onset of apprehension. Ulana washed her hands in heated water and started the examination.

"How long have you carried this child?" she asked through Deelia.

"About four and a half months."

Deelia relayed the answer, and when she finished, Leslie asked her, "Why did Ulana ask about the length of time? Can't she tell by looking?"

Deelia shrugged. "Should I ask?"

"Sure, maybe I'll learn something."

After a Rendille exchange, Deelia said to Leslie, "She sees that you've been bleeding."

"Yes. But she knew that when you asked her to come. It isn't serious, is it?"

"Ulana hasn't said one way or the other."

"That doesn't sound good. Ask her what the bleeding means."

Deelia, looking embarrassed, spoke to the midwife, but Ulana seemed to ignore the question. She said something that Deelia then relayed.

"Ulana asks if you've been feeling, how do you say, a tightness?" Deelia made gripping motions with her hands.

"What? Contractions?"

Deelia nodded.

Leslie thought. Contractions! Certainly there hadn't been any since the new bleeding started. On the camel or passed out in Gof's dwelling, who knows?

"I don't think so."

Before Deelia could relay the answer, Ulana pointed between Leslie's legs.

Deelia leaned to look.

Her eyes widened with surprise, and she sidled close to Leslie's face and whispered the words: "Ulana sees that you have not been circumcised."

Before Leslie could respond, Ulana spoke to Deelia. The Rendille women talked together then stared at Leslie.

"Deelia, ask her to tell me about the bleeding."

Deelia looked back at the midwife but said nothing.

Leslie waited. What would she do if they wouldn't talk to her? Both of them, unlike Wambila, seemed all hung up on circumcision.

To Wambila, the practice was barbaric and abhorrent. "It is a way for the men to control us," she'd said. "They use the ritual to remove our organs of pleasure. Then husbands can be as neglectful as they please."

Leslie's mind raced. What if they try to force it on me?

"Perhaps you are not circumcised because you are not Rendille?" said Deelia.

Leslie smiled and nodded an enthusiastic nod. "Yes, yes, of course. I am from people who do not do circumcisions on women. It is against our beliefs."

Deelia spoke a stream of words to Ulana. The midwife continued to glare at Leslie. It was as if she'd decided that, no matter what, Leslie was wanton and not to be forgiven. They all sat. In time, Ulana turned away and washed her hands.

"She isn't through, is she?"

Deelia didn't answer.

"Won't she even talk to me?"

Tears welled in Deelia's eyes. "I am sorry Lees-lee. I cannot help this."

"But..." The midwife wiped her hands and scowled once more at Leslie. Then she said a few words to Deelia and left.

Leslie crawled to the doorway and watched the woman go. She turned to Deelia who sat by the fireplace.

"Is there another midwife?"

Deelia nodded. "There is, but Ulana said that she will come back for another look at you."

"But she doesn't tell me anything."

"Next time, she may. Besides, the other woman would be worse. She believes even more strongly than Ulana in the traditional rules. You are better with this midwife, I think."

"But I can't communicate with this midwife."

"She will be better next time."

"How can you say that? Why would she be better next time?"

Deelia seemed uncertain, then blurted, "Ulana will be better with you, because Jeidid will tell her she must. She is his number two wife. She will obey him."

Leslie shook her head. What a mess... left alone, in this web of tribal traditionalists, and one man to appeal to... a man who is never here.

For the fourth time, the ravine widened. The warrior named Jaisut stopped the caravan, motioning for Firingin to come to the lead camel. Another junction in the trail, and the young man at the head of the train needed help.

Firingin put down his end of the carrying mat, and Hedad lowered his. Firingin walked to Jaisut and pointed to the well-traveled pathway heading south.

Hedad smiled when Firingin returned to his post. Hedad did not respect Jaisut.

While being carried, Karsi woke several times. Once he tried to get up, but the raising of his head seemed to distress him. He then laid back, moaning. He had lost much blood from his wound and needed to eat, but the caravan could not stop for a meal. Until it reached the open desert, danger of an ambush still remained.

The sun moved across the slit of sky, and the ravine filled with shadows. Night came, and patches of moonlight appeared at wide places in the canyon.

The procession moved without talking. Firingin searched the shadows for Turkana but saw none. The raiders seemed to have fled as Jaisut had said.

Hours after darkness, the walls of the ravine receded to ground level. The caravan moved toward the broad plain of the western Chalbi.

Outside the ravine, the warrior pulled the column to a stop.

"Move onward," ordered Firingin. It would be unsafe to stop so close.

The warrior obeyed.

The train of six camels continued for another hour, and Hedad needed a rest from the carrying. Well into the wadi, Firingin signaled for a halt. He approached Jaisut. "Here we will rest and eat."

Jaisut's teeth glittered with a smile.

"We will leave the beasts standing," added Firingin. "If the Turkana come, fleeing will be our best protection."

Jaisut nodded and took up his rifle. "I will keep watch. Even without bullets, my weapon will frighten the evil ones." Firingin nodded.

Jaisut left to take a post toward the canyon entrance, and Firingin looked for Kaido. He wanted the boy to do the cooking, but Kaido was not to be seen.

He must be hiding, thought Firingin.

Hedad came, running. He remained ready to help.

"Are you strong enough to unpack supplies for the meal?" Hedad nodded and opened the straps of the food container.

While the boy rummaged through the contents, Firingin drove a stake in the ground for tethering the lead camel.

"Only dates and millet remain," said Hedad. "And tea."

Firingin nodded. "It is sufficient. Now go make a fire for the cooking. Make it near the leader's mat. And make the pit deep, so the flames will not give a signal in the darkness."

A gust of wind ruffled the nearby bushes, the first stirring of the blowing that would come as the night air cooled. "Make haste," said Firingin. "The eating must be finished before the sand moves from the ground."

Hedad went to his work, and Firingin took fodder from the lead camel's pack and spread it for her. Behind the last beast in line, he saw the boy. Covered with a thick layer of dust, Kaido skulked behind the animals.

Firingin laughed out loud. "Kaido, you look as a ghost." Kaido moved behind a camel, and brushing sounds could be heard.

A strange boy, this young Wambile. "Come now. Ghost or not, you must help spread the fodder."

Kaido emerged, and keeping a distance from Firingin, he picked up an armful of feed and distributed it in front of the two unfed camels.

The smell of tea came from the cooking area. "It is time for eating," said Firingin.

Kaido nodded and followed behind him.

At the fire, Hedad poured two bowls of the steaming brew.

Firingin took one and nodded toward Karsi. "Has he spoken?"

Hedad answered that he had not. The warrior joined the group and sat beside Kaido. Hedad served the millet, and Firingin poured tea for Jaisut.

Perhaps smelling the food, Karsi opened his eyes and raised his body.

"Where is this place?"

The others looked to Firingin for the answer. They now relied on him for everything.

"We are out of the canyon. South, toward Hedaidile's village."

Firingin gave Karsi a bowl of tea, and the wounded leader sipped once. He tried to raise up and spilled hot liquid on himself. He fell back on the mat, and he groaned.

Hedad watched until the groaning stopped, then he handed the leader a bowl of millet. Karsi pushed it away.

"Has the lead beast been trained for riding?" asked Firingin.

The leader nodded.

"Then you must gain strength so you can ride. You must eat so the strength will come to you."

The boys both nodded their agreement and so did the warrior. No one wanted more carrying. Karsi tried the millet and ate a few bites. The evening wind increased, and surface sand churned into the air.

"We must start," said Firingin.

The warrior pointed toward the leader. "But, he is not yet strong for the riding."

"We cannot wait until he is strong. From here until morning, you must carry him, and Kaido must help you."

Jaisut winced but nodded to the order.

"And you must stay close to the camels. You must use your voices, so I may hear you. Clouds of dust will blow. You must not get lost in the darkness."

Before midnight, the wind roared to storm levels, but the caravan pressed forward. Firingin ordered Hedad to come from behind and walk at his side. Both kept watch on the two struggling with the mat. Stops were frequent.

After the skies cleared, Hedad went back to his post. Firingin walked alone and thought of Leslie and the trip they had made across this same desert. He wondered about her care in the village to the north and if he would see her again. A sadness came, and he felt water around his eyes.

Three days had passed, and Ulana had not returned. Deelia had brought tubers from the desert for Leslie, and served mixtures of cow's blood and milk. The spotting stopped. Then it started again, but it was less. Leslie's strength had improved, and she ventured out on another trip to the courtyard.

This time Jeidid stood with a group of the men. Leslie waited near the dwellings, and when his eyes showed that he saw her, she motioned to him. He seemed to ignore her. She took a step in his direction.

He came to her.

"What are you doing here?"

"I wish to speak to you."

"I cannot talk to you in this public place. You are a woman, not even a wife to me."

"But..."

He started to walk away.

"Wait, what I have to say is important. You are making a big mistake about the police, and..."

He stopped. "I will come to Deelia's dwelling tonight. We will speak of this then."

Satisfied that she would finally get to say what she needed to,

Leslie left. A group of women walking in the opposite direction from her stopped and looked.

She greeted them, and one, a younger woman, smiled and spoke in a friendly way. Gossip about Leslie being uncircumcised had no doubt made its rounds inside the village. By now, she was probably scorned or envied by every wife in the settlement. The woman who spoke must have been one who envied.

The men of the community?

Tribal custom, Wambila had once told Leslie, dictates that any woman who is not circumcised can be the object of love for any man. A married woman, however, has sex only by her husband in the traditional clans; if she is pregnant, even that is forbidden. Clearly, Leslie's condition had presented an overwhelming dilemma to the males of Kulal village.

That night Jeidid came, as promised, and Leslie sat waiting for him to invite her to start the conversation. Better to be patient, she thought, but Jeidid said nothing, and Deelia appeared to be upset.

He's here for one of his conjugal visits! Leslie realized, and suddenly embarrassed, she crawled toward the doorway.

"So, we'll talk later," she said to Jeidid.

He nodded, and when she reached the opening, he ordered her to wait outside. "I will talk with you there."

She crawled out and sat beside the entrance, but then another command came from Jeidid. "Speak now what you have to say to me."

Leslie's jaw dropped. Can this be the way he wants to do it... talking to me while he's...

A second command from Jeidid, and she obeyed.

"It's just that I wanted to tell you..."

She heard a moan from Deelia.

Jeidid's voice again. "Go on, what did you want to tell me?"

"Well, I thought you ought to know that the police will be coming for me. That they..."

"I already know this."

"But you announced..." Another moan.

"Anything else?"

"Then you'll be going to talk to the police, I suppose."

No answer.

"When you do talk to the police, I want you to tell them that I'm now ready to surrender. They don't need to come with there soldiers and their guns, I want to go back now. I want to go so I can testify at Firingin's trial."

"Impossible!"

She would have asked then what he meant by impossible, but a third moan stopped her.

How can anyone talk under such conditions?

"Have you another question?"

She wondered if she shouldn't end this right now, but knew she had to hear his answer. "I want to know what you mean by impossible. What is..."

"I cannot go to the police. The Turkana are between here and Marsabit."

Stunned by that, she said nothing.

Sounds of heavy breathing came, then once again Jeidid's voice.

"Have you anything else?"

Realizing that she might not get another chance to talk to this man, she decided to raise another of her topics. "I would like to show Deelia how to start a school."

"No!" screamed Deelia.

Leslie hesitated.

"A school?" said Jeidid. "What kind of a school?"

"Maybe I shouldn't..."

"Speak! What kind of a school would you have her start?"

"I thought, possibly, a school here in the village. For the children. To teach them reading and numbers. And English, perhaps..."

"I do not want this!"

Jeidid's voice. "Deelia does not want the school."

Leslie shook her head in the darkness. The conversation had become hopeless.

Jeidid again. "I will think on this school idea. Anything more you want to say?"

Leslie kept silent.

"What about your bleeding?"

Surprised, she reacted without thinking. "How did you find out about that.... Ulana! I suppose she told you."

"Deelia spoke of it to me. You have seen Ulana about this problem?"

Leslie nodded to the empty night. "Once. She was supposed to come back, but so far hasn't. I thought you might..."

"Ulana will come."

Leslie sat waiting for more, but the conversation had apparently ended. She crawled, to the far side of the dwelling. Minutes later, she saw Jeidid emerge and walk toward the courtyard.

She stayed, not moving, wondering how she could ever face Deelia. What can I say to her after something like that? Deelia did not come out, and through the remainder of the night, Leslie huddled, alone, by the doorway.

With the sunrise, the young woman came from the hut carrying her milking gourd. Leslie cringed, but Deelia seemed cheerful and smiled a blissful smile. "I am so happy, Less lee."

"Happy?"

"I am happy because Jeidid is so strong with love for me."

"But the talking about the police and..." She had stopped short of bringing up the exchange over the school.

"Yes, he talked to you of many things. But all the time he talked, he was sleeping with me."

Leslie looked away.

No big surprise when, later in the day, Ulana came. She smiled upon entering the dwelling and sat chatting with Deelia over a serving of tea. Not wanting to be the cause of another aborted examination by saying things, Leslie waited.

After maybe an hour, and almost as an afterthought, Ulana put down her tea bowl and crawled toward the bedmat. With a grin as broad as the desert sky, she then gestured for Leslie to remove her wrap and lie down.

The examination took but a moment. Deelia relayed the result. "She says you're bleeding less but still a little."

"Yes, I knew that, but what does it mean? Is my trouble over?"

Deelia spoke to Ulana, and Ulana answered right back.

"She says she has seen other cases when the blood was greater than yours, and the babies lived."

"Doesn't sound at all encouraging. Were the babies healthy? They lived, but were they normal?"

Deelia asked Ulana.

"The babies were healthy."

"And the mothers? Were they all right?"

"You must not worry," said Deelia.

"How can you say that? You haven't even asked her the question."

Deelia spoke to Ulana. Ulana's expression showed irritation, and she didn't answer.

"Maybe if I rephrase this. I don't mean to question Ulana's abilities, but can't I find out about the health of the mothers? Can't she, at least, tell me if the women were okay?"

Deelia looked hard at the midwife. Then she looked at Leslie. "Ulana will not speak of the mothers," said Deelia.

21

The tenth day after leaving the ravine, Firingin started seeing the familiar features of the southern country. Hot, open plains stretched eastward from the caravan's path, and to the south loomed the hazy tops of the Ndoto Mountains.

The procession had moved much slower than expected. Too many stops impeded progress. Once during a night-long storm, they'd gotten lost. The next morning they were far from the western hills and had to backtrack most of the day.

Details of nearby terrain now showed that the coming night would bring the caravan to the oasis north of Jeiso's settlement. Firingin smiled. Perhaps tomorrow, they would arrive at the village, itself.

"You are amused?" said Karsi from his perch on the lead camel.

Firingin turned and walked backwards. "I smile because of thoughts I carry in my head. I think of days from the past."

"Better days than these, yes?"

"That is so."

"You think of your woman?"

Firingin nodded. Karsi stated what seemed obvious. "In jail, you will not see her again?"

Firingin shrugged.

"And never the child it is said she carries?"

Firingin shook his head. He turned and walked forward.

Karsi continued. "But why is it you make this trouble for your-self? Jail is not a place for one as skilled as you. Your knowledge of beasts and your strength for leading others has saved our caravan. Soon you will be a hero among the Kulal people." Again Firingin shook his head. "Perhaps. But, I cannot accept such honor while my grandfather suffers."

Karsi said nothing. The driving of the wind and the plodding of the camels made the only sounds.

The boy Hedad came running. "A caravan!" he shouted. "It approaches from the east. It is Rendille, I think."

Firingin lifted his eyes and looked in the direction of Hedad's pointing. In the distance, he saw the shimmering images of twelve beasts and four drivers. The formation was that of a desert water-hauler.

"Your eyes are good, Hedad. I also see the men as Rendille."

Hedad smiled.

Firingin held back on the lead rope, bringing his charges to a halt. Kaido came from the follower's post.

"Why do we stop?" Behind the column, he had seen little but its dust and the rear flanks of the camels.

Karsi pointed toward the alkaline basin on their left. "We have visitors. Friendly, we think."

Kaido, ever fearful, cried out. "They move fast. Are they not Turkana?"

Firingin answered. "These are too tall to be Turkana, and they walk as Rendille drivers."

Kaido brushed dust from his hair and squinted at the oncoming band. The leader of the approaching group waved, and Firingin waved back. "These are from my grandfather's village. Their leader is my comrade from caravans in the past. Keigo is his name."

Within seconds, the arriving train of camels came alongside and shuffled to a halt. While the animals sniffed the air, and some bellowed, Keigo approached.

"Firingin!" he said. "Why are you here? We thought you were gone forever."

With a hint of pride in his voice, Firingin answered, "I come to free Jeiso."

Keigo looked puzzled, but offered no response to the words. He looked at Karsi, still on the camel, and the others, standing beside Firingin.

"Who are all of these?"

Karsi replied. "We are from the village of Mount Kulal. Our headman is Jeidid of the family named Wambile."

Keigo nodded. "Jeidid? Yes, I have heard the name." He regarded the train of camels. "You carry salt. But your caravan is small, and one of your beasts is without a load."

Hedad spoke up. "In a ravine, north of this place, we were attacked by Turkana." He pointed to Firingin. "This one, who you know, has saved us."

Keigo nodded but made no reply. He had never been one who conversed with boys.

He motioned to Firingin. "I would speak with you."

Firingin nodded.

Keigo walked to a place beyond the hearing of either group of drivers. Firingin walked with him. Keigo spoke with a low voice. "You have fought with Turkana?"

"The caravan was attacked."

"The boy said you defeated them?"

"Not me. The warrior, Jaisut, drove them away by the shooting of his rifle."

Keigo shook his head. "Not many have passed through the lands where the Turkana raid."

"We lost our other warrior, killed, and three of our boy-drivers were killed also. One beast was shot, and the Turkana took four others with loads of salt. Several beasts ran and were not found."

Keigo shook his head.

The two men stood silent. Then Keigo spoke. "This freeing of Jeiso, you say you come to do. I do not understand it."

Firingin stared at his companion. Could it be that a senior elder of the village did not know of Jeiso's capture?

"How many days has your caravan been away in the desert?"

Keigo shrugged. "We went only to Kargi. Maybe ten days."

"You should know, then, that Jeiso was taken by the police. That he is in jail in..."

Keigo held up a hand. "Jeiso was taken; that is true. But how did you hear of it?"

"Jeidid, the Kulal headman, he told me. He knew of it after a police raid on his own people."

Keigo nodded. "I heard the stories, in Kargi, about police raids in the eastern and northern villages."

Firingin thought again of the horror he had brought.

Keigo said more: "Jeiso was gone only five days before the police brought him back."

"He is not in jail!"

"He was in the village when I left."

Firingin said nothing. His feelings moved between joy for Jeiso and embarrassment over the now useless rescue.

Keigo continued. "The police took the old one to Nakuru. He told us of flying as bird in their machine. Five days later, when he came back, he spoke to the village, and proud as a king-lion, he told us that the Kenyans would not come again."

"Would not come again? But how can that be?"

Keigo stood silent, and Firingin spoke quiet words. "I must see Jeiso and learn for myself how this strange thing has happened."

Keigo smiled. "Your grandfather will be pleased to see you. When we heard of Turkana attacks in the north, we feared for you... and for your woman."

Firingin said nothing. With Jeiso already freed, it would be right to return immediately to Leslie, but first he would go to the village and talk to the old one.

Keigo's words continued. "Jeiso grieved over your death. He grieved for days. Then the police came, and when they brought him back, he said he would speak no more of you."

Firingin stared at the horizon.

Keigo had more to say. "Jeiso will want to hear about your battle with the Turkana. We, ourselves, no longer travel to markets in the lands controlled by them."

"What of the trading of your young beasts? This is the season when they must be sold for grain and water."

"We traded a few yearlings to Kargi, but the yards in that place are full. Buyers in Kargi will take no more of our animals. We need to go to South Horr and the other centers. But we cannot. Soon we will have to use shillings to buy water for the dry season."

Firingin scratched the ground with the toe of a sandal. Keigo stood, shaking his head. "And you, with one warrior and that group of boys would have tried to free Jeiso?"

Firingin frowned. "Those from Kulal are not here to free Jeiso."

"How, then, could you have even thought of doing what you say?"

Firingin did not answer.

Keigo smiled tight-lipped disbelief and once more shook his head. "Even with all the warriors of the Rendille clans, nobody could have done such a thing."

Firingin opened his mouth to explain but closed it again.

That afternoon and through the night, the two caravans traveled together. The following morning, they made a mass encampment by the spring where Firingin and Leslie had seen the Turkana with the donkeys. The joint meal was most festive. Karsi and the boys from Kulal talked with great enthusiasm to their new friends. Even Kaido spoke with pride of surviving the attack in the ravine.

Keigo's drivers served lamb and curded milk for the breakfast. The crew of the decimated salt caravan ate as they had not eaten since leaving their home village.

After resting a time in their tents, the drivers returned to their camels and the caravans moved southward. In late afternoon, the columns approached the collection of low huts that made up Hedaidile Village. The ragged band from Mount Kulal stopped outside the corral. They would wait for the customary invitation to enter.

The boys fed the last of the fodder to the camels, and the warrior helped Karsi down.

Firingin gazed at the village. Everything seemed as it had been, no obvious destruction from the police raids. As normal for the time of day, cooking fires burned, women and children busied themselves with evening chores, and corral workers stabled livestock for the night.

After a time, Keigo approached. "You will now bring your beasts inside. Then you will go to the courtyard, where Jeiso waits."

By the time Firingin and the boys had finished bedding down the camels, darkness had come to the village. Voices murmured over the meals inside the dwellings.

Firingin walked directly to the central circle of huts and stopped in front of the structure that belonged to Jeiso's number one wife. The old one sat by the doorway, wrapped in a blanket.

A hand extended from the blanket, and a familiar voice rasped, "Greetings, Grandson. Have you eaten your nightly meal?"

Firingin touched the hand and nodded. "I ate with the drivers."

"I would offer you a smoke, but she is within. I must not disturb her." The senior woman of Jeiso's family remained powerful as ever.

"I have no need to smoke, Grandfather."

Jeiso patted a place beside himself.

Firingin sat.

Jeiso pulled the blanket tighter. "It is cold on these nights."

Though it did not seem cold to Firingin, he did not contradict. The two sat in silence.

Firingin thought of his need for answers but said nothing. He would honor Jeiso's desire for waiting.

After a time the old man spoke. "Your woman? She is alive?"

Firingin nodded.

Jeiso again: "She still carries the child?"

Once more Firingin nodded. He wasn't certain of Leslie's health in the pregnancy, but he would not trouble Jeiso with speculation.

"Keigo tells that you came to free me."

"I was told that you were taken by the police."

Jeiso coughed and cleared his throat. "The police are fools." Jeiso spoke the words, but his former vehemence had left. "The police are fools, but they are strong."

A hand moved in a wide arch. "As a bird, I flew in their machine, over the tops of great mountains. Below, I saw beasts and men as insects. From above the city of Nakuru, I looked down on dwellings with square corners. Some sat on top of other dwellings, and I saw machines that growled and ran over the ground." Jeiso did not know that Firingin had seen such dwellings and machines—many times.

The old man paused, staring at the distant hills. Then he added, "It is a great power that the Kenyans have, greater than any Rendille or Samburu. You must not fight such power, my grandson."

"Yes, I know this."

"But you came with only boys to free me. You cannot even think of such things."

Firingin shook his head. "The boys are drivers for Jeidid's caravan. They would not have fought the Kenyans."

"Jeidid, the great man of the north. Your woman stays in his village?"

Firingin nodded.

"I told the Kenyans that you and your woman were dead. How could I know otherwise. The Turkana kill many. You went alone among them with only the woman and two camels. I could not stop you."

A coughing spell shook Jeiso's body. Firingin waited.

"I am pleased that they did not kill you, but the police were pleased when I told them that you were dead. I think that such knowledge saved them from having to tell their headman that they could not find you. They were not pleased when I told them of the woman's death. They call your Leslie 'the tourist.' A strange name for a woman. They had hoped to send her back to her people."

Firingin would not interrupt with explanations.

Another spasm of coughing, and Jeiso continued. "After he heard that you and the woman were gone, the one named Chief Inspector Wanja, a Kikuyu I believe, said the matter was finished. He then ordered the metal bands they had placed on my arms to be taken off, and with his flying machine, he brought me back across the desert." Jeiso grinned showing all the teeth he possessed. "That one, Chief Inspector Wanjau, told me that the police have no desire to keep a great headman such as me from my people."

With all of his questions answered—all except how he would now tell the answers to Leslie, Firingin stood to leave.

Jeiso motioned for him to stay.

Firingin obeyed, and they sat in silence. Jeiso let his eyes close.

Firingin thought of another question

"It is said, Grandfather, that before the police took you, you fought them with a knife."

Jeiso said nothing.

"Jeidid told me you fought bravely."

"I fought as one who is weak. I drew no blood... Only made loud noises and struck at the air with my poor blade."

"The knife...it was not..."

"The jeweled knife was hidden. It remains so today... in the desert."

"But why is it now hidden when the police will not return?"

"I leave the knife in Wak's care. When I die it will be found and placed with honor beside my body."

"But who will know where to find the weapon?"

Jeiso stared a long minute. "You, my grandson. Now that you are here, I will show you where it is"

Not expecting such an answer, Firingin looked away.

After a long silence Jeiso spoke again. "The trading, this season, has been bad for me. The markets in Kargi will take no more beasts, and we still have a great need for water."

"Keigo has told me of this."

"The Turkana have made it so. They keep my caravans from South Horr and the other places. I have few drivers and warriors to fight them."

Firingin offered no response, and Jeiso spoke again. "Keigo tells me that you and Jeidid's boys fought the Turkana in the great canyon."

"Our caravan was attacked by them."

Jeiso nodded. "Keigo said that you drove the bandits away."

"The Kulal warrior who is with us killed one and frightened the rest with his shooting."

"Keigo says that one of the drivers has come wounded to my village. I am told that the injury makes it necessary for that one to ride."

"It is Karsi, the caravan leader, who is wounded. He cannot walk far, but each day he grows stronger."

"I will have a woman who is a healer look at his wound, and he will stay in my village until he is well."

"I will tell him of your generosity, but he may not stay as you say. His caravan has salt that must be delivered to South Horr."

"I will buy Jeidid's salt for more shillings than those bandits in South Horr will pay. And I will also pay for the use of his camels."

"For the use of..."

"You and the warrior who shot the Turkana will join my drivers and Jeidid's boys to make a caravan that will take my yearlings to the southern market in Korr."

Firingin stood and stared at Jeiso. "Grandfather, I must go to Leslie. The child, your great-grandchild, will soon be born."

Jeiso dismissed Firingin's words with a wave of a hand. "No one goes to the north. If you tried, you would be attacked again. You cannot go to her until the Turkana are no longer there."

Firingin looked toward the distant sky. It would be more than four months until the birth of the child. Perhaps the Turkana would soon leave.... four months would allow plenty of time for one caravan to help Jeiso.

Probably because he sensed that his point had been made, Jeiso stood. "Go now," he said. "Tomorrow we will talk more." He then leaned close to Firingin and whispered, "This night, my grandson, you may lie in the bed of a soft woman of my village."

Firingin looked to the north and thought again of Leslie.

Jeiso continued. "Hedad's widow comes often to my wives and speaks of her desire for you."

Firingin remembered the pleadings of Hedad's wife in the days after her husband's death. "This night, I will sleep in the corral," he said.

Jeiso ducked toward the doorway. "Do as you wish, but Jessina would make a good lie for you. I, myself, have seen how eager she is."

Firingin walked away and did not answer.

22

L ying on her mat and waiting for sleep, Leslie felt her baby move for the first time. She sat up to tell Deelia, but the young woman was already deep in slumber. Leslie wiggled once— a small celebration. How she wished Wambila were near to share this moment.

She thought of Firingin. Where would her baby's father be on this night? In jail, perhaps... maybe worse! He'll never feel any of his child's movements, never know anything about its birth or its growing up....

She tried to think of something else. Ulana came to mind. Why wouldn't the midwife answer about the mothers? Had those women died? Maybe death during childbirth is what usually happens? Leslie shuddered. She needed to see a real doctor, one who worked in a modern facility. She'd depended too long on Gof and Ulana, those caught up in a traditional neglect toward female patients.

The desert around here stretches, maybe, hundreds of miles to the nearest town, she thought. Even if I could get my hands on a camel and a driver, I couldn't dream of riding that far. The police, and their helicopters, are the obvious answer, but Jeidid won't go to them—because of the Turkana, he says. The next chance I get, I'll try again to persuade him. Firingin and I made it past the Turkana. Why couldn't he with all the warriors and camels he must have.

Days passed with no sign of the village elder. Leslie made repeated trips to the courtyard but never saw him.

Deelia was having her period--always a bad time for her. But more than that, the magic after Jeidid's visit two weeks earlier was now over. There had obviously been no conception, and wailing and general lamentation filled the air around the small dwelling. Leslie tried to tell Deelia that Jeidid was, no doubt, sterile, but that only made her hostess angry.

When Leslie next saw Jeidid, it was the night of a scheduled conjugal visit. She crawled outside as soon as she saw him and took a position for waiting far from the doorway. There would be no more conversations through the walls if she could help it.

Jeidid spent but a few minutes with Deelia, and when he came out, Leslie walked up to him. "Jeidid! I must speak to you."

He turned away.

"It's important, a life and death situation." She hated using such a dramatic phrase, but she had to get his attention.

He grimaced. "What situation?"

"I must see a doctor."

He looked concerned. "You have a new illness?"

"No, not really. I just need a doctor who understands pre-natal care and how to deliver babies when there are problems."

Jeidid glanced to the sky, annoyed. "You have care for the birth of your baby. Ulana is the best midwife in our village."

"But she...she seems to think...or says that..."

"Please, I do know wish to hear of women's things. Ulana will give you the care you need."

"I don't want Ulana!"

His eyes showed a hint of anger, but Leslie would not be deterred. "I believe there is great risk for me here. I must be taken to a place where I can get modern medical attention."

Jeidid looked alarmed for a moment, then smiled and shook his head. "Your husband paid two camels for you to be cared for in our village. He has been given a promise, by me, that we will give you what you need."

"I know, you told me that before, but I need better attention than I'm getting. I need somebody who knows what to do when things aren't going right."

His gaze drifted in the direction of one of the nearby huts, the darkened dwelling of Ulana. "You say that things are still not going right?"

"No, they aren't, or at least I don't think they are."

As if seeking escape, he looked back toward the entrance of Deelia's dwelling. He quickly looked away.

"I need someone who can diagnose my condition," said Leslie. "A gynecologist who can prescribe exercise, and the right foods and medicines."

Jeidid grinned. "Ulana, she frightens you."

"No, not frightens. Well, maybe that is it. She just doesn't seem to have enough experience with someone like me."

He almost laughed. "Your women have babies the same way as ours, don't they?"

She hated hearing him come with the same sarcasm she'd used on the midwife.

"Never mind Ulana," she said. "I have a simple request that has nothing to do with her—well, not directly."

He grinned at her fumbling.

"What I want you to do," she added, using her most authoritative tone, "is to try to make contact with the police. You can get through, I'm sure. Firingin and I saw only a few ragged Turkana when we came north, and they really didn't seem like they could do much...."

Jeidid's expression turned serious.

"You understand my words?" she said.

He nodded. "I understand that you wish to return to America."

"No, not necessarily."

Lord, is that what I have to face—raising my African child in the United States. "I just want medical care. I'm married to a

Kenyan. I should be able to..."

"Your husband is a prisoner. Or soon will be. You cannot stay in Kenya because of him."

"So, you think I'll be deported."

"I do think so."

He smiled. "I will talk to Gof. He will help you with foods and medicines."

"Shit!"

"You voice a complaint?"

"Yes, a complaint. I don't want Gof and his sleeping potions."

"But why do you complain? Gof attended you well, I think. You came to him almost dead with fever and he cured you. He is the best doctor for all things. He will care for you now, and soon you will have your baby. Then you will be as a girl again."

Startled by his last remark, she stared at him.

"A girl again? What does that mean?"

Jeidid raised a hand. "Please, dear lady, I will argue no longer. It is decided."

He left, and Leslie sat down in the darkness, her frustration replaced by curiosity and also apprehension. What game is this head elder playing? Why is he so reluctant to help me go to the police? He must know it would be the best thing for me, and it's bound to be best for the safety of his village.

It occurred to her that knowing she wasn't circumcised— everyone knew that by now, he might want to keep her around until after the baby was born—to have sex with her.

"That's absurd," she mumbled to herself. "The heat of this desert is affecting your brain, Leslie Halstrom."

The following afternoon, while sitting with Deelia in front of the dwelling, Leslie looked up and saw Gof approaching.

He looked different. His costume had changed. Most of the feathers were missing, and he had replaced his skin loin-wrap with one made of patterned black and white cloth.

He stood before them and spoke Leslie's name. Or at least it sounded like her name.

"You'd better go," said Deelia. "He might go inside if you don't."

Why the spirit man should not enter Deelia's hut, Leslie couldn't even guess, but she wouldn't ask either. She stood, apprehensive but also hopeful. *It's possible, of course, that Gof has come to tell me that he doesn't handle pregnancies.... Possible, but not likely.*

Gof smiled—it seemed that even his teeth were cleaner. Cautiously, Leslie smiled back.

Gof said nothing but pointed in the direction of his own dwelling, and he started to walk. She hesitated. Her eyes searched for a route of escape. Faces peeked around nearby dwellings. The episode seemed a spectator event to at least some of the villagers. Knowing escape would be impossible, she followed Gof.

Outside his doorway, she again hesitated. The healer's painted, right-arm stretched back, and a finger beckoned. She crawled inside and was immediately ushered to the patient's mat and directed to sit.

Squatting near the doorway, Gof studied her, perhaps wondering if she would bolt as soon as he moved. She stared at his hands. His fingernails had been missed in his new bent toward a sanitary life. *How could she possibly let him examine her.* He moved closer.

"No," she said. "I don't need to be looked at. Ulana has already seen me." He nodded. Then he started wailing a low, sing-songy chant.

At his fireplace, liquid boiled in a scarred pot, and without interrupting his singing, Gof filled a bowl with the bubbling brew and handed it to Leslie.

She set the bowl down. "I don't want to sleep."

Gof broke his chant, uttered a loud woof at her. She picked up the bowl, and he resumed the wailing, now even dancing, hunkered down like a Russian Cossack.

She sipped a little of the tea.

He kept dancing, and she sat and watched. This time, the tea didn't make her sleepy.

Gof's performance was indeed magnificent, but she wondered if all his chanting and hunkering might not be his way of facing up to the new, and perhaps unsavory assignment he'd received from the village elder.

Suddenly, the man of spirits stopped and reached in the pouch at his waist. With a string of woofs, he withdrew the animal bones and bits of skin.

In his crouch, he rotated once and threw the items on the floor. Then he stooped low and stared at the result.

Silence.

Leslie looked at the ceiling to keep from laughing.

Gof crab-walked over and sat by her head.

His face cracked—literally because of the dried paint—into a smile.

"Good news?" she joked.

He didn't laugh but nodded and started to talk.

She held up a hand. "I don't understand you. Please speak slowly."

His Swahili words came one by one. "You..will... bear..a.. well...child."

He looked proud and seemed to be waiting for her reaction.

"Okay. Suppose I believe you. How about me? Will I also be well? I've been bleeding you know."

He nodded.

"So, you know? Or it won't be bad for me?"

He looked alarmed. So convincing was his expression, she herself felt concerned.

"How..." She wouldn't ask him that. How could he know anything from those bones and skins?

"Bad?" he said.

"Bad? Yes, will I be well like the baby, or will I be..."

He shook his head vigorously. "You will not be bad. Gof will watch you and will keep you good."

She smiled and drank the rest of the tea.

Each day she drank tea and ingested mixtures prepared by Gof. The bleeding stopped completely, and she gained strength. She felt the baby moving more and more, and in time, she stopped thinking about any need for modern doctors. With Gof's herbs and the rich food Deelia supplied, she felt better than she had felt in months. She even started helping Deelia with chores in the mornings and evenings.

The baby grew, and Leslie's body grew. She began to feel the joy of becoming a mother, and basking in her newly acquired strength, she spent hours strolling about the village.

Curious about those from other parts of the desert, she stood near groups of visiting herdsmen and tried to hear their stories.

She listened for mention of Firingin. Though it seemed to her that his surrender to the police should have been a big topic of conversation, she heard nothing.

She once asked Deelia why Firingin's sacrifice was never talked about. Deelia answered that none of the herdsmen this year came from the southern regions. "Because of the Turkana, the men with animals come only from the north. They know nothing of police raids or of the capture of Jeiso Hedaidile."

Leslie then realized that nobody would be coming from Jeiso's village—not for a long time.

Her use of the local language improved, and Deelia invited her to come to the village circle where women sat in the mid-morning, grinding millet and stitching garments.

The women talked, gossip mostly, but some asked Leslie about her previous life. She told them, as best she could, about Jeiso's village and a little about America.

The women were interested in everything she said about the people in the south but seemed not to believe her accounts of the cities, freeways, and airports of the United States.

She considered saying something about the starting of a school, but decided against it. It wouldn't be wise to raise the issue unless Jeidid was for it, and she'd heard nothing from him on the subject.

Often, the Turkana were discussed, and once Leslie mentioned the encounter that she and Firingin had experienced.

The grinding and sewing stopped, and all the women listened. "You and the man Firingin were alone," asked one of the women.

Leslie nodded.

"Why then did the fierce ones allow you to live?"

Leslie started to answer, but she was interrupted by a loud shriek from a different woman.

"You are a ghost!" screamed the shrieker. "Your skin is pale as the milk of a summer cow. You have come from the dead and are here to bring us evil."

Several woman screamed and all but Deelia turned away from Leslie.

"I cannot be a ghost," pleaded Leslie. "Look! Do you see how my belly grows. A Rendille baby grows inside me. Ghosts do not grow Rendille babies."

The circle buzzed, and most of the women nodded to the logic of Leslie's words. Leslie added, "My husband, the man Firingin, has the eyesight of a night-leopard. He saw the bandits before they saw us. We did not die. We hid in a ravine until the Turkana were gone."

Some of the women grinned, and all returned to the grinding and stitching.

That same afternoon, Leslie and Deelia sat in front of Deelia's dwelling scraping hair from a camel-skin. Leslie looked up and saw Jeidid approach. His face had a solemn appearance, the look of a man on an unwanted mission.

Deelia bowed and spoke. "Welcome, my husband. What brings you to us?"

"I would speak with Leslie, and we must speak alone."

Deelia stood but didn't leave.

"Go!" shouted Jeidid.

Deelia bit her lip and marched as a disciplined child across the yard.

Jeidid sat beside Leslie.

She thought of his promise to think about the school. "I've be wanting to ask you..."

He held up a hand. "I am here on behalf of the village elders."

"The village elders?"

"Yes, we have all decided that you must know what we know."

"About what?"

Again he raised a hand.   "Wait and I will tell you."

She waited.

"This morning, one of the herders from a neighboring clan told us of a conversation he overheard in Loiyangalani."

"The town by the lake?"

Jeidid nodded. "A town frequented by Turkana."

She said nothing.

"The conversation the Rendille man heard was between two Turkana warriors. One bragged to the other about a caravan that had been destroyed. The bragger talked of a Rendille caravan that he and others had captured during the season of the last quarter moon."

"About a month back."

Jeidid nodded. "More like five weeks. The attack took place in the deep canyon south of Kulal. That canyon is four or five days' travel from here."

She did the arithmetic. "You think...?"

"I fear it is so. The Turkana said it was a Rendille salt carrier accompanied by warriors."

Her question came with a husky voice. "Were there survivors?"

"The bragger said there were none."

She shivered.

Jeidid touched her arm. "I fear it is now unlikely that someone comes for you from the south. Another caravan must go to them before they can know that you are here."

She looked long and hard at Jeidid. "Aren't you going to send someone to find out what happened?"

"In time, perhaps."

"Some might have gotten away. The Turkana bragger could have been lying."

"Please. The Turkana rarely leave survivors. There will be nothing recognizable to be seen. By now, the scavengers of the desert will have done their work on the remains."

"But there might be something—damaged cargo or broken weapons?"

He shook his head. "After the Turkana raids stop, I will send a caravan. They will see what is there."

"But you expect nothing?"

"I expect nothing."

Suddenly feeling lost and alone, she struggled to stand. Without knowing where she would go, she needed to walk.

Jeidid reached across to help her up. She pushed his arm away.

Powdered with dust and loaded with baskets of Rift-Valley millet, the line of twenty camels moved across a lava-marbled basin east of Ilaut. Men and animals of this second expedition in three months from Jeiso Hedaidile's village groaned as they labored over ridges of the razor-hard ejecta. Firingin, solemn with the responsibility of leading the massive column, walked tall and straight at the front.

"I need you to be the leader," Jeiso had said after Firingin had agreed to help with the previous caravan.

Firingin had resisted. "I should not lead. I will go on only one expedition for you, and when the caravan returns, I will leave your village and travel to where my woman waits."

"Your woman does not wait," countered Jeiso. "She thinks you are gone forever."

"True, she does not wait for me, but she looks for someone from your village to come, a column to bring her here. She has said she wants to live in this place, and now that I do not go to prison, I must be the one who goes for her."

"Bah! You worry too much about that female."

The force of Jeiso response surprised Firingin.

"The woman is alone..."

"She is not alone. Already, she has found many friends among the wives in Jeidid's village. She is a woman. Women always find friends."

"The child will be born; I should be there."

"You cannot help your woman when the child comes. Bearing children is not the business of a man. The baby will be born the same if you are there or not. Stay, and lead caravans for me, and when you go to your wife, you can show her the wealth you have gained. You can then give her and the child status—no man can do more for his family."

Firingin had not thought before of gain and status, but there were many things he did not understand about the business of being a Rendille elder. His grandfather had wisdom of such things and had spoken with great authority.

The first caravan had traveled for more than a month. It had delivered young camels to Korr and had brought back loads of clean water.

After returning to the village, Firingin had made plans to return to Kulal. He'd inquired about Turkana raiders, and Karsi, who had stayed behind to gain strength and complete his healing, had told him that the threat remained.

"Three days ago," he'd said, "a column of camels made the trip to the northern spring to bring water to the village. They returned without the loads because the drivers had seen Turkana with rifles in the hills."

Firingin then decided to wait and Jeiso had a new project in mind. "I need you to take a caravan to the markets in South Horr and then to the wells in Korr," he said.

"But I must go to the north as soon as the Turkana have left."

"They will not go so soon that you cannot do one more favor for your grandfather and his people."

Firingin could not reject such a plea. "I will go for you," he said, "but South Horr is not a safe direction. The Turkana do much of their raiding between here and that town."

"I do not fear Turkana with you as the caravan leader."

Firingin shook his head.

"The caravan will not be loaded when it goes," explained Jeiso, "and it will not take young beasts for trading. The column will move fast, and the Turkana will not catch it."

Firingin frowned. "If you do not send camels, what will we sell on this trip?"

Jeiso grinned. "You will take shillings to the markets in South Horr."

"Shillings?"

Jeiso ignored the reaction, and looking first to see if anyone watched, he reached deep in his robe and brought forth a large wad of paper money. "I will now give you sixty-thousand of these from my own wealth."

He handed the shillings to Firingin, and Firingin held them, peeling back one or two of the top bills.

"Put them away," whispered Jeiso. "People must not see how much money I have."

Firingin stuffed the notes into one of his inside pockets. "But this is most of your treasure, Grandfather. I fear the trust you place upon me."

"It is most of my wealth, that is so. But you must not fear, my grandson. You are the strongest and most honored member of my family. You are the only one I can bestow with such responsibility. I know you will keep my money safe, because you have already shown that you will fight anyone who attacks you."

"But Keigo is..."

The patriarch held up a hand. "Keigo is old. He is weak, and his mind is forgetful. I cannot trust Keigo with large numbers of shillings. If you had not returned to our village, we would have been made poor by the threat of the Turkana. We would have been forced to live on the water from our single well and what little we might have brought from the northern spring. It was a great favor from Wak when you came to us."

Jeiso's words about Keigo were indeed strange from one perhaps ten years Keigo's senior, but Firingin would not object. He held the bundle of bills tight inside his pocket and looked away toward the western sky.

"What is it I will do with your shillings in the market of South Horr?" he asked.

"You will use the money to buy thirty-two baskets of millet from the grain trader. Keigo will help with the talking. His thinking is weak but he still has a good voice."

"The Kenyan police are known to be in South Horr."

"Do not worry about the police. The Kenyans now believe you to be dead. This I have already told you."

"But they may learn otherwise if they see me before them."

"They will not be looking for you alive and dressed as a Rendille elder."

It is true, thought Firingin, the police will not look upon me as the one they seek. I no longer appear as the Samburu boy they have searched for. The black goatskin cloak is gone, burned on a fire and replaced by my orange wrap of flowing cloth with deep folds at its seams. My bone ear-pieces are also gone, and I now wear metal ringlets hung, one from each lower lobe. My herdsboy's necklace has become a single strand of white beads, a thin metal bracelet circles each of my wrists, and my head, is shaved as that of a senior Rendille. I appear as a man from an important desert clan, a person who will not be questioned by the police or any other I might encounter.

He nodded to his grandfather's assurances. "And where is it I will take the millet I purchase in South Horr?"

"You will sell most of it in the community of Korr. You will sell all but two baskets for thirty bags of Korr's water. And you will also get back shillings for the grain you sell, more than the sixty-thousand you now hold. You will bring the shillings, the water and the two baskets of millet back to my village, and when you do, I will make you richer than any man you know...." Jeiso showed the gaps of his teeth in a smile. "Richer than any man but me."

Realizing the expedition's great importance to his grandfather and to the village, Firingin had gone forth from the meeting and without wasting a day, started to organize the caravan. More than two months remained until the date when Leslie's child would be born, but Firingin knew that time on a caravan can disappear as milk from a leaky gourd.

He ordered the warriors who would be along to practice shooting with their rifles, and he had Jaisut show him how to work such weapons. He and Jaisut shot jackals, and he felt a sorrow at seeing swift, wild lives so easily ended.

Before leaving Jeiso's corral, all but two of the caravan's camels were loaded with empty baskets and flattened water bags. The lead animal and one other carried food and tents for the large entourage of drivers and guards. When the column departed, Jaisut carried his shooting weapon at one point in front. Three armed warriors from Jeiso's village marched at other positions. Though no Turkana had been seen on the previous caravan to Korr, Firingin would not take chances carrying Jeiso's shillings on the dangerous route to South Horr.

Karsi had joined the party of drivers. Rest and care had brought him back to good health, and he had been anxious to return to the trail. The two boys from Kulal also took places with the column. The procession was arranged in a normal in-line formation with drivers on either side and more behind. Keigo, glowering and silent, walked ten camel lengths to Firingin's right. Behind Keigo walked the boy Kaido. Fearful and longing for his home in the north, Kaido scowled into the glaring sun. To Firingin's left marched Karsi and behind him, the one named Hedad held his body erect and proud. Ever watchful, the boy with the name of the heroic cousin attempted to copy all of Firingin's movements. Behind Hedad and Kaido followed two drivers from Jeiso's community. Trailing in the cloud of dust were two more.

The trip to South Horr was swift and uneventful, and trading at the market went well. Keigo might be old and feeble in Jeiso's eyes, but more than talking was used by the senior elder to save twelve thousand of the paper shillings and still load all the baskets with high quality grain.

After South Horr, the caravan traveled in daylight and rested at night. The camels were kneeled but not unloaded. With loud bawling, the beasts complained under their carriers. Three drivers were required on each watch to keep the cargo from being spilled by restless animals.

At the evening meals, talk was lively. When he wasn't on watch, the boy Hedad sat close to Firingin and asked questions about things seen during the day.

"The donkey with stripes. Why is the creature marked that way?"

Kaido crept close to hear, and Firingin tired from his responsibilities gave a short answer. "The animal was a zebra."

"A zebra?" asked Hedad. "Why have I not seen such a creature before?"

"Hedad, you show yourself as a child," responded Karsi. "Any one from our village who is old enough to go to the mountain has seen such animals. On the high slopes those animals live along with other grazing creatures. And hunting beasts also live on Kulal. Once I saw a leopard in a tree near the ridge between the two peaks."

Hedad looked away, embarrassed. Kaido let a smile nudge at his lips.

On the night the caravan camped near Ilaut, Hedad asked about the mountain, nearby.

"Baio is its name," said Firingin. "A caravan leader with name the same as yours, a great man who is now dead, told me of the mountain."

Hedad looked somber and said nothing.

After the warriors and the young drivers went to their bedrolls, Firingin and Keigo sat by the fire.

Keigo spoke. "You talk with great admiration for your lost cousin?"

Firingin nodded. "He was a wise leader and a good friend."

Keigo produced a toothy smile. "Hedad always had a story to tell and a song for singing."

"It was his way."

Keigo looked at the night sky. "It is said that Hedad's widow is poor and lonely."

Firingin poked at the fire. Sparks rose from the embers. "Jeiso tells me I should take Jessina as my second wife."

Keigo nodded. "I have heard that he favors the marriage. But, I have also heard that you spurn Jessina. Why is it you will not go to her? She is a beauty to be sure."

"That she is. But my respect for Hedad makes me feel the guilt."

Keigo shook his head. "There are few men left in the village who would be of an age to marry Jessina. You must know that Hedad would not wish his widow to be unhappy and to live without the comfort of a husband."

Firingin thought on Keigo's words. It was true, Hedad would not wish the woman to be lonely.

At Korr, three days were needed for the grain to be sold and for the water to be loaded. Firingin rested and dreamed of his future. When I return to Jeiso's village, I will become the owner of, perhaps, ten or more camels. A second wife would be a symbol of such wealth, a way to increase my status in Jeiso's family. Perhaps I should marry Jessina, but I cannot until I have talked of it with Leslie. Her ways are different. I must not act without her permission.

When Keigo reported the water all loaded, it was near sunrise on the fourth day. A few hours sleep, a meal of roasted lamb and cooked millet left the drivers, with rested minds and full stomachs; ready for the trip home.

With the eighty thousand new shillings tucked under his wrap, Firingin thought of the child that would soon be born to Leslie. If a boy, he will become the inheritor of the wealth I will soon have. Leslie will wear the cock's-comb hair, and she will be much honored among Rendille women.

Firingin desired to tell his wife of the good fortune and vowed then that he would go to her without delay, no matter what reports had come about Turkana in the north.

24

News of the massacred men and boys traveled quickly around the village. Mothers wailed their grief for dead sons. Other women joined in, and for nearly a week the mood stayed glum.

Deelia moped inside the dwelling, and Leslie, with new realization that she would never again see her husband, sobbed as she wouldn't have thought possible. It was almost a relief when Ulana came stooping through the doorway.

The midwife, who looked as if she'd rather have been somewhere else, pointed at Leslie and uttered a string of hard-to-understand words.

Deelia clarified:

"She says she has come to examine you."

"Examine me—why?"

Deelia shrugged.

"I thought it was Gof who cared for me."

Deelia relayed the message and the answer.

"She says Gof cannot bring the baby. Men do not bring babies, she says."

Leslie shook her head.

Ulana, with a look of professional intensity in her eyes, washed her hands and ordered Leslie to disrobe.

Leslie obeyed.

Ulana squinted and probed, and when she looked up, she smiled and spoke to Deelia.

Deelia relayed: "There is no bleeding. There is no sign of trouble."

"That's good to hear. Did she happen to say how much longer it will be?"

Deelia asked but received no reply.

"What about Gof?" asked Leslie. "Should I keep seeing him for the herbs and such?"

Deelia asked and received only a shrug from the midwife.

"I guess I'll keep seeing him."

The next time Leslie visited the spirit man, he gave her a new kind of dried leaves to crumble into her daily bowl of millet. "Make strong," he said.

She didn't know if he meant she should take a heavy dose of the leaves or if the new herb would make her strong.

She asked, but Gof only grinned and nodded his head.

Whatever he meant, it seemed to make him happy. The time must be short, she told herself. At least he thinks so.

Leslie grew to enormous size. Deelia told her she could stop helping with the heavy work, and Leslie used the extra time to formulate a new plan for her future: She would again ask Jeidid to send for the police—not right away but soon after the baby was born. Paranoia over lechery aside, she couldn't believe the head elder wouldn't want her and her child to be gone from his village. With Turkana raids seemingly a thing of the past—no mention in the morning circles of recent attacks—he shouldn't have any objection to sending someone.

When the police come, Leslie reasoned, I'll tell them that my baby is a Kenyan citizen.... But they should be able to figure that out when they see how new he is. As the mother, I shouldn't have any further trouble with deportation. Even the police ought to be sympathetic to a child needing its mother. Once that's all settled,

I'll have the officers fly me to Jeiso's village, and from there I'll see if I can testify at Firingin's trial.

Leslie next saw Jeidid one morning when she was on her way to the village well for water. Across the courtyard, he nodded and left the group of male talkers to come to her.   She stood and waited.

Shamelessly, he looked at her huge belly. "Your child will be here soon?"

She ignored his comment. "Can we talk?"

He motioned for her to sit in the shade of a small tree. "We can talk there. The elders will allow it because of your grief over your husband's death."

She shook her head. "It isn't Firingin's death I want to talk about."

He smiled. "No matter. The elders will not know what we say to each other." He pointed again to the patch of shade.

Once more she shook her head. "I hate to be so contrary, but sitting is not for me if I can help it. As big as I am, it's much easier if I stand or walk."

He took a step in the direction of the well. "You are going for water?"

She nodded.

He smiled. "I will walk with you, and perhaps you will allow me to carry the gourd when it is filled."

What is going on here?

She thought of asking him, but he spoke first. "Soon it will be that you are as a girl again."

So that's it. She stopped and stared at him. "Listen! I don't know what you mean by that line. But if you're thinking... "

He held both hands in a surrender pose. "I mean nothing other than a concern for the discomfort you must feel. It is your first child is it not?"

"Yes... But what you said sounded like..."

Jeidid's grin stopped her in mid-sentence.

"What is it, then, you wish to talk about?"

She started walking again. "I don't know... Maybe it ought to wait."

"As you wish, but the elders will not allow many opportunities such as this."

"It's just something I've been thinking about. Plans for after the the baby is born."

His face grew somber.

Leslie continued. "What I want, is for you try to get a message from me to the police. Not now but after the baby is here."

"You mean for the police to come and get you?"

"Yes."

He shook his head. "It is not wise, but that I have already told you."

She nodded. "Yes, you have..."

He'd held up a hand. "I know. After you have the child, you will want to take it back to America."

"No, not to America. I just need to talk to them. To tell them about the baby... tell them that Firingin is dead and they can stop raiding the villages."

"The police already know of his death, I think. They hear the talk of the Turkana the same as we. There have been no helicopter attacks anywhere in this region since before your husband left."

Surprised by his words, she stared blankly for a moment, then replied, "But, I still need to talk to them. To explain that he killed the soldier in self- defense... that he was trying to return me to the tour group..."

Jeidid interrupted.

"But the police also want you, I believe."

"That's true. But, I can persuade them not to deport me. You see, by running the school in Jeiso's village, I was performing a valuable service for Kenya. I'm sure they'll be happy to let me stay after I tell them I want to continue that service."

He smiled. "I think the police will send you to America."

"I don't think they will, not when they know I have a child whose father is Kenyan."

A smile spread across his face. "You are a crafty woman, but I fear your plan will fail."

"Fail! Why do you say that?"

Jeidid looked toward the far horizon. "The baby's father is dead. Even its grandfather is in jail. The baby's Kenyan lineage is weak. You, in the eyes of the government should not be here. I believe they will send you back to America... but without your baby."

"You're crazy... "

Jeidid's expression showed alarm.

"I don't mean crazy... really. It's just an American's way of saying you're completely wrong in what you say. Since I'll be the baby's mother..."

Jeidid raised a hand. "I do not know all the rules, but it seems likely that the baby will stay with Jeiso's family. The baby will stay and you will be returned to your own people."

"You're mistaken," she interrupted. "I think the government will let me stay too. When I tell them that I want to raise my Kenyan child in its home village.... That I want to reopen the school for the children..." She paused. Once again, a smile from Jeidid had stopped her.

"I think you presume too much about the Kenyan police. They only know that you should not be here, and they will send you away."

Now showing teeth in a wide grin, Jeidid said, "I did not know that people of your race believed in impossible daydreams."

"You just tell the police to come, and you'll see how much I'm dreaming."

"After your baby is here, we will talk again. If you still want it, I will try to send for the police. They are in Marsabit, and it will take time to reach them, but I might be able to get a messenger through. Turkana raids have mostly ceased in that direction."

"So, you'll do it? You'll send for the police?"

"Wait until your baby comes. We'll talk, and if you still want me to send a messenger, I will try."

When the contractions first started, Leslie didn't even notice.

She'd been working through an old lesson plan, trying to convert the Swahili to Rendille, and diverted from thinking about her pregnancy, she hadn't identified the light spasm as anything unusual.

The second feeling of tightness came so long after the first, she made no connection between the two. With Deelia away doing chores, she found the water jar empty and had started walking to the well. Before she reached the spring, the third cramp hit and brought a pain so intense that it caused her knees to buckle. She grabbed the wall of a nearby dwelling and hung on for support until the agony passed. Then she hurried as fast as she could to Deelia's hut.

Deelia sat in the back of the dark room, stirring up a mixture of blood and milk and looked up with alarm when Leslie crawled through the doorway.

"Get Gof," gasped Leslie.

Deelia stared a moment, not moving.

"Go! Get him quick. Something is happening."

"I'll bring Ulana," said Deelia, and she rushed out the dwelling.

A few minutes later, another strong pain. Leslie laid down on her mat, and moaning, she tucked her knees toward her chin.

When Deelia came back, the midwife wasn't with her. "Ulana says you must wait until the pains are close."

Just then another came, and Leslie screamed.

Deelia sat with rounded eyes and watched. When the pain subsided, Leslie yelled, "Get Gof. And don't come back without..."

Deelia had already left. When she came back, the spirit man followed close behind.

Immediately, he started brushing dust from an area of Deelia's floor.

"No!" Leslie shouted. "There's no need for your bag of tricks. Just give me some herbs or something for this pain."

Gof paid no attention. He cleared a circle and woofed two times before throwing his skins and bones. He inspected the pattern then quickly went to Deelia. He spoke a string of unintelligible words to her and then came back to sit by Leslie's head.

"Baby comes," he said.

Over the months, he'd apparently given up on his quest for a sanitary life. The smell of him almost made Leslie vomit.

He looked at her, waiting it seemed.

"Do something," Leslie wailed, "or else go away."

Gof continued to sit, appearing to be immobilized.

Another pain, and Leslie screamed again.

Gof sidled to the far side of the room and spoke again to Deelia. Deelia left.

A short time later, Ulana, clearly upset, entered the dwelling, and Deelia followed.

Gof sidestepped to a place by the doorway.

Using a scratched piece of mirror, Ulana peered between Leslie's legs. Then she spoke to Gof.

"What does she say?" Leslie asked Deelia.

Deelia answered, weakly, "She says he shouldn't call her again until you are ready."

Another contraction, more intense than the last. Leslie let out a loud scream. By the time the pain subsided, Ulana had left.

Gof remained, huddled in his corner.

Through the day he stayed and watched. Clearly, he knew nothing of bringing babies into the world.

Leslie's contractions increased in duration and intensity. Deelia stayed close and squirted cool water on Leslie's forehead.

Hours into the night Ulana came back to the dwelling. Immediately, she had Deelia hold an oil lamp while she leaned down for a look. She sat back and spoke to Deelia.

"Now, what does she say?" asked Leslie.

"She says I should heat water. And bring sheets of cloth for your mat."

Ulana looked over her shoulder and apparently saw Gof. A look of disgust came over her, and she motioned for the spirit man to leave. Silent as vapor, he obeyed, and even before the gesture of dismissal had been completed, he was gone.

Ulana got down to business. She washed her hands and arms in the heated water and then washed Leslie. Several more contractions. Ulana waited through them. She held the lamp and inspected between Leslie's legs. After one of the inspections, she touched Leslie on an arm and pointed to herself. Then she acted out a process of pushing down and breathing. She gripped her hands together and spoke directly to Leslie.

"You... tight..." Ulana squeezed her hands. "You push baby." She relaxed her hands. "You not tight... You..." She demonstrated taking deep breaths.

Another pain came and passed, and Ulana rolled Leslie to one side while Deelia spread a cloth and laid a hairless skin over the foot of the mat.

Both attendants waited—Ulana again holding the lamp.

The contractions started coming less often, and Ulana motioned for Leslie to sit up.   Another demonstration. Ulana squatted with her knees spread wide. She pointed to the middle of the mat and repeatedly nodded her head.

Leslie hesitated.

"She wants you to take that position," said Deelia. "She says it will bring the baby faster."

Leslie tried. Bulky as she was, it wasn't easy to get into a squatting stance.

Another contraction. Ulana made downward pushing motions with her hands. Leslie pushed and felt the baby move. She pushed again, and Ulana ducked forward with open hands.

The midwife looked up and smiled.

More pushing and breathing. Exhausted, Leslie fell back on the mat. Ulana made her sit with her knees held high. Leslie obeyed but felt she could push no more.

The contractions kept coming. Suddenly Ulana laughed.

A tremendous feeling of movement, and the midwife sat back and lifted up a small bloody object.

"Your baby!" shrieked Deelia. "It is out of you."

Ulana spanked the child on the bottom, and just like on TV, the baby let out a lusty cry.

Deelia grinned. "It is a boy. Your baby is a boy."

Almost ready to pass out, Leslie nodded. "I always knew it would be."

Ulana laid the baby on Leslie's flattened tummy and ordered Deelia to bring more water.

The midwife worked methodically cutting and tying the umbilical cord.

When the placenta came, Ulana ordered Deelia to clean it up and to make another change of the sheets. Then the midwife sat down heavily by the fireplace.

Drenched in perspiration, Leslie laid back and regarded her son.

It seemed almost unreal to see him, this stranger who'd been so close to her for so long, the human being she'd be related to from this day forward. No more would she live a life without family. She'd be called mother by this one she now beheld for the first time.

"His name?" asked Deelia. "What will you call your light-skinned son?"

Leslie smiled. She had, of course, thought of names for her child. If it had been a girl, she'd always known it would have been Jean, for her devoted aunt.

Firingin would not have wanted his son to have his name. Her husband had hated his Samburu name. If he had lived, he'd would have probably changed it to a name connected to Jeiso's family, maybe Hedad.

"He shall have his grandfather's name," answered Leslie.

"Jeiso?" "

No. He will be Eric, the name of my father."

She reached forward and touched the baby. "Eric Halstrom Hedaidile, a mouthful but that will be your name."

Ulana spoke up. "We must tell Jeidid."

"Why? What does he have to do with it?"

"He will make a record of your child's birth, and when he next visits Marsabit, he will give a name to the child."

"But I've already named my baby. Didn't you hear? Eric. The child's name is Eric Halstrom Hedaidile."

A shroud of detachment came over the midwife's face. She crawled to the doorway. Before she left, she looked back and smiled. "Jeidid will decide."

25

Shouting and dancing with joy, the villagers assembled by the corral to greet the returning caravan. The boy driver that Firingin had sent ahead told them of the column's approach and also told of the success from the trading at Korr. The news had spread quickly, and after more than two months of waiting, the people rejoiced. They would now have water and fresh millet for their needs. Wives and mothers who had worried about the safety of their husbands and sons could laugh again and sing.

Firingin lead his trail-worn charges through the happy crowd and then ordered the unloading of the camels.

He went to Jeiso. A series of sandstorms had stretched the trip from Korr by more than two weeks, and he needed to tell his grandfather that all the camels and men were safe.

The old one sat, grinning when Firingin arrived in the courtyard. He stood and held his arms open. Firingin approached, and Jeiso spit greetings.

"Welcome home, my grandson."

Firingin spit back, and the two men stood smiling.

"All the animals and drivers are well," he said and reached into his inner pocket. He drew forth the huge wad of shillings. "The water is being unloaded, also the millet."

"A success beyond my hopes!" replied Jeiso. "I have ordered the slaughter of four bullocks. This night, there will be a feast in the village."

Jeiso took the money and counted out bills for ten thousand shillings. "Take these as payment for your good work."

Firingin felt emotion pull a tightness in his throat. "Your generosity is great, Grandfather."

Jeiso waved an arm. "Now, go and see the beasts that wait for you. You will find the size of your new herd to be greater than you have dreamed."

Firingin moved both hands as if fending off an attack. "You give me more than I deserve."

"I give you nothing. You have earned these things by your skill and your courage."

Realizing that further protest would be futile, Firingin spoke of a needed condition on the transaction. "Before I accept your payment, I must tell you that one beast will be returned to you. I must replace the she-camel that you loaned me for the trip to the north. I had to sell that beast to Jeidid for the keep of my woman and the child."

Jeiso smiled. "No matter. You may give back a beast if it pleases you, but go now. See the rest of your wealth. Find a woman and dance with the dancers. You are, as you were when you came back from Hedad's expedition, the hero of our village."

Firingin turned to leave, and he thought of his need to tell Jeiso of the trip to Kulal.

"I must speak to you, Grandfather, of my leaving to go to Leslie."

Jeiso scowled. "Today is for celebrating. The feast is waiting. Go! Tomorrow we will talk of these other things."

In the corral, twenty-five beasts, each with two notches in their ears, were shown to Firingin. Five of the animals were newly marked: they were the lead camel and four others from the caravan Firingin had just brought from the desert. The remaining twenty were young animals that Jeiso must have purchased while the caravan was away.

Firingin asked Heiso, the man who showed him the camels,

where the new creatures had come from.

"They were brought here by Samburu for the purchase of women from our village. Thirty-five camels and ten bullocks were delivered to our corral as the payment for three marriageable girls."

"Thirty-five camels and ten bullocks? That makes a great price for three girls."

"Uncircumcised and without fathers, five maidens were offered to the Samburu, but the elders from the Ndotos spurned the two who were older."

Firingin sensed that Heiso's answer would be long, but he would not interrupt.

"Jeiso showed much anger over the rejection. He sulked and fumed and threatened to force the men from the south to leave with no women at all."

Firingin smiled. There was mystery in Heiso's tale.

"While Jeiso fumed, the Samburu found time to enjoy the sex of the younger girls. Jeiso, hearing of it, told the elders that they could take the three females they wanted, but only for the price of all five...."

Firingin laughed out loud. As in days past, when the trading of Firingin's pregnant mother had fooled her Samburu husband, Jeiso had shrewdness when it came to selling women to men from the southern clans.

"So here are your beasts," concluded Heiso and led Firingin in front of the line of standing camels.

Firingin walked past the group, giving a close look only to the new animals. They appeared healthy and sound of limb. He pointed out the lead camel from the caravan and ordered her returned to Jeiso's herd.

Heiso obeyed, first bobbing the creature's tail as a new marking. Firingin left the corral.

He had thought much of the woman, Jessina, since he and Keigo had talked. He would now go to her dwelling, and if she was within, he would ask her to come to the celebration, and perhaps, during the festivities, he would learn of her qualifications for becoming a wife to him.

He walked past the courtyard, and he heard sounds of drumming and the ringing of bells. Smoke from the pits where meat cooked wafted over the village. The merrymaking had already begun.

At the doorway of Jessina's hut, he leaned down and saw the woman inside. She sat near her fireplace and scraped hair from a camelskin.

He greeted her, and she looked up from her work. "I would go with you to the feast," he said.

She looked wildly about as if confused. "You wish to go with me?"

He nodded. "It is a celebration for the return of the caravan. People will dance, and there will be meat from bullocks."

"I do not understand this," she said. "In the past, you have not wanted to go anywhere with me. Why do you now want to take me to a public place."

Why does she question my motives? thought Firingin. He felt reluctant to explain to a woman why he did things, but he would offer an answer to this one question.

"I have thought of you while on the caravan. I wish now to know you better."

She smiled in a way that made him want her at that moment, and she crawled to the doorway and looked toward the music. "I must prepare myself. I must not go to a place of eating and dancing, wearing a wrap that smells of camel's oil."

She looked into his eyes for a long moment.

"Come," said she, "you must wait inside while I don my finest wrap."

His pulse made pounding in his ears, but he would not place himself within the sphere of her powers. He waited outside while she made herself ready.

The following morning, Firingin awakened with sunlight shining on his face. He had celebrated with Jessina until after the midnight hours, eating and dancing in the courtyard. He had danced little in his previous life, only at his wedding to Leslie, but Jessina's excitement gave motion to his feet and strength for the jumping with the young warriors. He'd drunk fermentation of mash mixed with camel's milk. His heart and tongue had loosened, and he'd said many things to Jessina. He remembered speaking of love and wondered if he had spoken of marriage.

Jessina had left the dancing before morning, saying that she needed to sleep before it was time to get up for chores, but Firingin had stayed. He drank more with the drivers and the warriors, and in the glow of sunrise, he had stumbled his way to a bed of straw in the corral.

He now rose from the place where he'd slept with a family of goats. The fermentation in his body made his head feel heavy and full of water. He dunked himself in the trough where the beasts drank. He felt better.

Heiso waited nearby, speaking of care for the camels.

"See to it," grumbled Firingin, and Heiso nodded.

Firingin remembered his need to talk to Jeiso, but first he would find Jessina and ask her about his words at the party.

When he saw her, she was coming back from milking. She appeared joyous and energetic.

"Firingin," she trilled, "I am surprised to see you awake so early."

He replied with a strong voice. "I would speak with you."

She mocked him with a bow. "Come, have your morning meal in my dwelling. We may speak there."

"I do not need food."

"Come, and we may speak while I prepare millet for myself."

He did not want to watch her cooking, but he needed to talk.

Inside the low structure, she placed the gourd filled with goat's milk near the fireplace.

"Do not cook," he said. "I have no appetite for the smells of cooking."

She motioned him to the blankets in the back, but he waited by the doorway. The looseness of her wrap revealed the curves of her body, and he felt the urging. He sat rigid. He must not give in to this temptation.

"Now, what is it you wish to talk about?" cooed Jessina.

He shook his head. "I will come back another time, a time when my head is clear, and I can say what I want to." Then he backed himself out of Jessina's doorway.

Jeiso ended his game of bau and stood to greet his grandson. "Did you enjoy the celebration?"

"Too much, I fear," answered Firingin.

Jeiso smiled a liquid smile. "I saw you with Jessina. In the night, did you take the pleasure of her body?"

Firingin scowled and did not answer.

Jeiso pointed to the dwelling behind him. "Come let us go where we may talk without the ears of others."

Firingin followed his grandfather to the abode of Jeiso's senior wife.

"I have sent her to the desert to search for firewood," said Jeiso. The two men sat facing. Jeiso stoked the bowl of his water pipe, and Firingin hoped the smoke would not bring sickness.

Jeiso leaned across. "Now tell me of your night of pleasures."

Firingin looked past his grandfather to the open doorway. "I come only to speak of the trip I will soon make to Kulal Village."

Disappointment clouded Jeiso's face. "You will not even gladden an old man's heart with a tale of excitement on a woman's blankets?"

"I remember dancing and eating and drinking. There was happiness in that, but now my head is full of pounding, and I wish not to speak of it."

Jeiso shrugged. "And you wish to face the Turkana so you can go to your white woman?"

"I will travel with the ones who are from Kulal, and we will take Jeidid's beasts and the shillings you paid for his salt and the use of his camels."

"It will be a trip with great risk."

"We will travel a path through the Chalbi. There have been few Turkana attacks in that direction."

Jeiso nodded and drew a puff from the hooka. He handed the stem to Firingin.

Firingin waved it away.

Jeiso nodded. "How long will you be gone?"

"It will be but a short time. I will not stay in Kulal. I will bring the woman and the child as soon as they can travel."

"You would return alone with them?"

"Leslie and I traveled alone when we went north. The Turkana do not waste their fury on those who carry little of value."

"I will send two warriors with you."

Firingin shook his head.

"I wish it," said Jeiso. "Those warriors will go to gain knowledge of Mount Kulal. In days to come, they will go back to Jeidid's village with beasts I send to graze on the high slopes."

Firingin understood and would not argue further.

Living as a Rendille woman, Leslie had little chance for a long convalescence. Two days after the birth, Ulana came to the dwelling and ordered her to be on her feet, walking, and with little Eric tight in her arms, Leslie started making slow treks around the compound. Women she knew greeted her with broad smiles and excited chatter. Leslie stopped and proudly showed them her new son. Morning circles were not to be avoided. Holding the baby, Leslie sat with a fold of sheep-fleece between her legs and did her best to mash kernels of grain with her free hand.

Sometimes while she sat, Eric nursed. She and two other women in the group breast-fed their infants. Rarely had Leslie seen any baby in the village fed by hand. In the few cases where it had happened, the newborns had soon grown weak and once the child had died.

It had been a relief to Leslie when right away Eric started taking sustenance from her rather than from a skin-covered gourd. The relief had been great but also there had been unexpected satisfaction. A primitive satisfaction, to be sure, but a completely fulfilling and delightful affirmation of self-worth.

The women in the circle talked often of her baby, his light color and his grayish eyes. Many could hardly form the European sound of his name. Ear-reek, it came from those more successful.

When Ulana sat in the circle—she was often away because of her midwifry—she stared at Leslie and the child. It was a look that could only be seen as pure resentment. What, Leslie wondered, is driving that woman to so much hatred?

Jeidid was not around. More duties on the mountain, no doubt. Leslie wondered if he would keep his word and send for the police. She definitely wanted it and had no reason, really, to believe the village elder would not do as he'd said. She discounted Ulana's threat about Jeidid picking the baby's name. It would be Ulana's way to make up such things.

Perhaps two weeks after the birth, Jeidid appeared at Deelia's dwelling for one of his conjugal visits. Leslie, as usual, scurried to her post outside. Holding Eric close, she sat in the coolness of a moonless night and hoped her baby wouldn't cry out at an inappropriate time.

After the usual, short, stay, Jeidid emerged. He stood and looked at Leslie and her son. He smiled. "I would see this child."

She rose to her feet and opened her wrap to expose the small face.

"He looks like his mother."

She looked down at her baby as though she hadn't seen him before. She'd never thought he looked like her. Someone in her family, perhaps, or maybe like Firingin.

An awkward silence.

Jeidid started to leave.

"Wait," said Leslie. "I'd like to know if you will be going to Marsabit... like you promised."

Jeidid looked toward the distant hills. "You still want me to bring the police?"

"I do. It's time for me to straighten out these false charges against my husband and to get back to Hedaidile Village."

"You want these things, even when you know you will never see your husband again?"

"Yes. I want to go to the place where we lived together and restart my life... open my school again."

Jeidid nodded. "Ah yes, the school." He looked toward the central part of the village, then shook his head. "It is a busy time on the mountain, but I may be able to get away... perhaps in several weeks. Still, I must tell you that I do not believe the Kenyans will respond as you expect. As I have said before, I think they will make you return to your homeland, and without your child."

"And I still think you're wrong about that. No one could be so heartless as to send a mother away from her infant baby."

Jeidid held up a hand. "Please, I know more of the ways of Kenya than you do. Your son is valuable to this country. He is valuable to the Rendille people. I do not believe the government will let him go."

She pulled Eric close to her and glared at Jeidid.

"I see that we must speak of this another time," said the elder and walked away toward the courtyard.

"Jeidid!" she shouted.

He kept walking.

Two days later, Leslie made her way from the circle of women and along the edge of the central plaza, heading for Deelia's hut. She was in a bad mood. Eric had cried constantly while she'd sat with him at the gathering. A hard rain in the night had left the ground moist and the winds calm. Flies had collected in swarms. She'd tried to keep Eric covered but hadn't been able to. In Deelia's dwelling, she hoped, smoke from the fire would drive some of the tormenters away.

Hurrying with her head down, she hadn't noticed Jeidid until he called to her. She looked up and saw him leave the group of men he'd been with and walk in her direction.

She stopped and waited. Perhaps he had something to tell her about going to the police.

What he said as he approached seemed to confirm her optimism. "I want you to know that in one week I will start on a trip to

Marsabit."

"Good." She brushed a hand over Eric to shoo away a gathering of insects. "Another day like this, and I'd have started out myself."

"But I will not be going there because of you."

"Oh?"

"The elders have reminded me that I must report the names of people from the village who have died, and those who have been married and also the children who have been born."

Remembering what Ulana had said about the naming of babies, Leslie scowled. "Still, you will see the police while you're there."

Jeidid held up a hand. "I will be going to the main government office. The Kenyans require reports every six months, but Turkana raids along the routes to the south and east have kept me from giving them for nearly a year. The officials in Marsabit know about the raids, but such attacks have now ended. I must go as soon as I can."

"But you will take my message to the police, won't you?"

"I can see them, but I have another, perhaps more important, thing to explain to you."

She stiffened. "A more important thing? What?"

The last time Jeidid told her an important thing it had been the announcement of her husband's death.

"What you need to know is that the child in your arms will be registered along with the others who have been born."

Oh, oh! He's going to tell me about changing Eric's name.... Ulana was right.

Jeidid watched her with patient eyes. "You see the problem, don't you?"

"I guess so. You're going to change my baby's name."

Jeidid shook his head.

"I have no right to do that, not the way things are at present."

"What does that mean?"

Jeidid didn't answer, and his expression offered no clue.

"Look, why don't you just skip reporting Eric's birth? It's only been a few weeks. Wouldn't it be better to just tell the police that I'm here, that I have a Rendille child and want to talk to them?"

"I cannot leave Eric out of the report. If the government were to find out about him later, it would be bad for all of us...especially for you."

She shooed another batch of flies from the cloth over the baby's face.

"And you really believe the Kenyans would send me back if they knew I was here... and they'd keep my child?"

Jeidid nodded.

"But if I don't turn myself in, what then? My husband is dead. Nobody is coming from Jeiso's village."

Jeidid smiled.

"Let us go to Deelia's dwelling. We can talk in private there."

"In private? Isn't that against the rules?"

He smiled again. "The elders know that I have a need to talk to you."

"But, you're already talking to me."

He took a step toward Deelia's lodge. "Come."

"Won't Deelia be there. She didn't go to circle this morning."

"I have sent Deelia to dig tubers in the desert. She will not return until chore time."

Now curious but also a bit nervous, Leslie walked behind Jeidid toward the low hut. Once inside, she prodded at the coals in the fireplace. Flames erupted and drove smoke and clouds of insects toward the hole in the roof, and opening the wrap over Eric's face, she sat down on her bedmat.

Jeidid, sitting on the opposite side of the fireplace, looked across with steady eyes.

She felt uncomfortable. She'd always considered him to be a nice looking man, but at that moment, he exuded an aura, an attitude of power perhaps, that made him look as dashing as any man she'd seen.

"I suppose you need information about Eric for your report? ...That's why the elders..."

Jeidid shook his head.

"So what is it you want to talk about?"

Jeidid looked toward the doorway. "I wish to propose a solution to your problem."

"A solution..."

He held up a hand. "With your husband dead, you are a free woman."

"Hardly. I can't go anywhere. I sit here chasing flies and waiting for God knows..."

"You are free to marry again. That is what I mean. Marriage after a spouse dies... it is even allowed in your country, I think."

"Yes, but I'm not interested in any..."

She stared at him.

"You mean you're asking me to be one of your wives?"

"It would solve your problem. Your child could become my son. I, one of the most powerful of all Rendille elders, would give you and Eric my family name. Unlike your former husband, I have no trouble with the police. Our marriage would be legal, and you would be entitled to stay in Kenya as my wife and as the mother of our child."

She sat, mouth agape.

Jeidid grinned and said nothing.

"But, I would be your fifth wife. It would be a harem with me as the lowest one."

Jeidid shook his head. "I cannot have children. You must know that by now."

"Yes, I have noticed."

"I've talked to the doctor at Marsabit. He says I have no disease, but my problem cannot be determined without more tests."

"So..."

A look of embarrassment came to Jeidid's face. "I cannot do such tests. It would not be possible for me to face my elders after doing such things for a Kenyan doctor."

She wondered at his shame but also thought of the torment carried by Jeidid's involuntarily barren wives.

He continued. "If you and I were married and I adopted Eric, your son would become the inheritor of my fortune, and you would become the most honored woman in all of Kulal Village."

Leslie's mind reeled. First threatened with a forced separation from her child and now offered marriage and status as queen of the village.... It was all too much.

She jammed a knuckle in her mouth and thought.

Jeidid waited.

"I can't even consider what you're proposing," she said. "I know next to nothing about you. In my country, people usually know each other before they marry. They spend time together."

He nodded. "I am aware of these things. It would be good for us to... how is it?... get acquainted. But time grows short. I must declare a name for your son, and you already have seen that it will bring problems."

"I have?"

"Perhaps I should finish my explanation. When I list Eric's family name as Hedaidile, the police will surely come... not to talk with you but to take you with their soldiers."

"Just because of the Hedaidile name?"

"I fear it is true. Hedaidile is not a common family in the Kulal region. While the police appear to have given up their search for you and your husband, knowledge of a child with that name, in this village, will certainly bring their helicopters."

She said nothing. Often, in the months that she'd been in this community, she'd wondered about the motives and the honesty of this man who now proposed marriage to her. Yet, she couldn't ignore what he'd been saying. Even the tour guide she'd had before being captured had told of the labor-intensive character of the Kenyan economy—of the need for the government to keep workers from leaving. It will be years before Eric is a worker, but I can't ignore the possibility that he might be forced to stay. If the police come here or anywhere else in Kenya where we might be, and they discover me and Eric.... I can't just sit and wait for that to happen.

"I need to think about this," she said.

Jeidid smiled. "Perhaps I will delay my trip for a few days. The Kenyans in Marsabit know it is a busy time for us at Mount Kulal."

Four days into the Chalbi and no storms had come. In
the evenings the winds were calm, no nighttime cooling to stir
the air over a desert that stretched to the limits of human vision.
Without relief from the oppressive heat, the camels carried their
heads drooped, their necks bowed forward. Each step had become
a challenge for both beast and driver.

Firingin, in front, was guided by the arc of sun in daylight and
by the bright star of the north at night. He would travel toward the
star for seven days and then turn so its light came over his right
shoulder. If he did not see the two humps of Mount Kulal after
three more days, he would steer his charges southwest, hoping to
approach from the northern direction.

The caravan, six camels being returned to Kulal and two more
that belonged to Firingin, carried no cargo. Light loads, forage for
the animals and provisions for the drivers, made travel through the
heart of the Chalbi possible.

Men and camels slept but three hours, each day, in the coolest
part of the mornings.

Talk was almost non-existent. Only the boy Hedad seemed to
have energy and imagination to speak words during the mostly si-
lent periods of eating. His talk was always of the same thing: the

return to his home village and his family. No one welcomed his conversation. When he approached, his eyes searching, warriors and other drivers set their mouths and glowered.

At first, the two warriors from Jeiso's village had grumbled about being assigned to the expedition, but now they were silent like the others.

No Turkana and no one else had been seen.

Jaisut complained of touching the hot metal on his rifle. Firingin allowed him and the one warrior from Jeiso's village who carried a rifle to stow their weapons on the lead camel.

At the beginning of the trek, Karsi had said that the caravan would cross the main route from northern villages to Kenyan towns in the east. No evidence had been seen of any thoroughfare, but the glare of unrelenting sunlight might have obscured the markings.

Karsi carried twenty thousand shillings in his pockets. They were payment from Jeiso for the salt and for the use of Jeidid's camels. Karsi and the others from Kulal Village were assured of their welcome, but Firingin was not. The people in Jeidid's community would not expect him. Though police attacks had been stopped, the people of Kulal Village might not know. They might fear to have him among them.

He did not care about the fears of the people of Kulal Village. Now a man, a wealthy elder, he would not hang his head before Jeidid or his people. He would tell Leslie of his success, and she would honor him. If a boy, his child would know great status among all Rendille clans.

Only one thing now caused Firingin concern. He did not know how he would talk to Leslie of a marriage to Jessina. He would tell her of the privilege of being a first wife with another woman to serve her. He would tell of the respect she would have in Jeiso's village. He would tell her many other things, but he did not know how he would face her questions and her anger.

Late on the fifth day in the desert, the sand started to lift in swirls from the level floor. The camels sniffed and bellowed, and Firingin looked hard at all parts of the sky.

To the south, the white glare had dimmed.

He halted the caravan and told Karsi to bring the camels from the rear and to make a circle for protection.

"You fear a storm?"

"It will be here soon. You must hurry and do as I say. I will drive a stake and tie the lead beast, but you must bring the others and call in the boys and the warriors."

Karsi left and Firingin pounded a long shaft deep into the sand, and before he felt the firmness of solid ground, dust began to fill the air.

"Hurry!" he shouted in the direction of Karsi.

More blows with the hammer, and he felt strong resistance. He pounded until the ring on the stake was less the a hand's width above the surface. He made the lead rope fast and looked back toward the column. Like visions in a ghostly vapor, the drivers and beasts came forward through the haze.

He kneeled the lead camel and caught the next animal in line. He pulled that one down. He would build a camel-barricade against the sand and debris.

Karsi came and hunkered at Firingin's side. He screamed to be heard over the howling wind. "I have ordered all to come. All except Jaisut. I did not find him at his post."

Firingin stood. "I must look for him."

Jaisut, the warrior who had fired his rifle and chased the Turkana, was also the one who could not follow trails. Jaisut would be lost in blowing sand.

Working his way back along lead-ropes and the flanks of camels, Firingin met the boy drivers and Jeiso's warriors, all crouching and pulling on spooked beasts.

"Good," he shouted as he passed. "Go to the front and wait with Karsi."

Even Kaido, the last in line, showed the face of determination. Firingin asked him if he had seen Jaisut. The boy did not seemed to hear. Firingin stepped away from him and into the storm.

Enveloped by curtains of airborne debris, Firingin moved with hands up, reaching for anything solid.

Again and again, he screamed Jaisut's name. No response.

Now lost himself, his only compass the direction of the wind, he kept staggering onward.

Branches, torn by the gale from bushes or trees in the vastness of the Chalbi, battered against Firingin's body. He knelt and turned his back to the onslaught.

Within minutes, the storm passed. The winds calmed to a serene silence, and a coolness settled across the land. From mounds of sand, smooth and suggesting a peaceful simplicity, men and boys emerged.

Firingin flailed his way to the surface of his private covering of desert material. He looked for the caravan and felt surprise when he saw it so close.

He called out the name of the lost warrior.

No answer.

He lifted himself from the sand and brushed the grains from his head and his clothing.

Another shout for Jaisut.

Again, no answer.

He walked away from the others, calling as he went.

Silence.

He returned to the train of camels. No one spoke.

Firingin's mind was filled with images from the day when his cousin Hedad was lost.

Karsi gave a report. "The boys, Jeiso's warriors and the beasts, all came through without injury."

Firingin stared and said nothing.

"What are your orders for us?" asked Karsi.

"We must find Jaisut. We must search for him...

Make a camp in this place. We will all look until Jaisut is found."

A marriage of convenience. That's what it would have been called in America. After getting over the initial shock of Jeidid's proposal, Leslie had thought long and hard about the offer. She couldn't just sit and wait for the police to come—that she'd already decided. And going to them no longer seemed like the right thing to do.

When he came to talk to her a week after the proposal, another day when Deelia wasn't at home, Leslie had already made a list of conditions for accepting. He sat across the fireplace from her, as before, but this time, it was she who directed the conversation.

"Supposing I agree to your arrangement, " she opened. "How can I be sure the things you promised: the wedding, the adoption of Eric, and him becoming the inheritor of your wealth will actually take place.

What if the elders object? What about your wives, Ulana and the others?"

Jeidid smiled. "I have already discussed the wedding and adoption with the elders. They all agree that it is best that there is a son to inherit my fortune."

"And your wives?"

"They have nothing to say about my affairs. If you agree to

marry me, our wedding will take place before I travel to Marsabit with the reports, and my wives will have no choice but to accept it. Most of them do not object, by the way."

She nodded.

"And you can put off your trip until after we are married?"

"I would put it off, because I wish to register our wedding along with the others that have occurred. Eric's adoption might take awhile longer, but I can start the necessary process while I am at the government office."

"And his name won't be a problem? I still want him to have Eric Halstrom Hedaidile in his name."

Jeidid shrugged. "His adopted name must include Wambile, for my family. With that one primary for him, I see no problem explaining the others. I will simply tell them that they were picked by his mother."

"So you promise you won't change his first three names?"

"I will not change them."

"And you don't think Hedaidile will bring the soldiers?"

"Not when you are my wife."

"But you'll have to explain how you met me, won't you? Since I'm the one they've been trying to get deported."

"If I have to, I will tell the officials that you came sick to our village from the desert, that we cared for you, and your baby was born among us. If they ask about Firingin, I will tell them that I heard he is dead."

"They will be satisfied by that, you think?"

Jeidid gave a patient answer. "They will, because it is true. And by the time I talk to them, you will already be one of my wives, and that will make you a Kenyan citizen. The orders to deport you will no longer apply."

"Okay, I accept that, I guess, but now I have something else I need to talk about—my school."

"You want to have a school in our village?"

She nodded. "I had one in Jeiso's..."

Smiling, he interrupted. "How can I object to something as

good for my people as a school? Of course you can have one here."

"But I need more than just permission. Some of the mothers may be afraid, so I will need your support, and I will need supplies. Will you buy the supplies I need when you go to Marsabit?"

"Make a list. I will buy what I can. And you can tell any mother you talk to about the school that I want it."

"And Deelia, I will need her to help me."

"Deelia will help."

This is going pretty well, thought Leslie, hope I'm not forgetting something. She referred to her list. "Oh yes, one more thing."

Jeidid grinned. "Only one more thing? I was beginning to think you would soon ask for your own grazing rights on the mountain."

She waved away his jest. "This is serious... something really important.... I'm not circumcised, you know? You've no doubt heard gossip about it?"

His expression turned somber. "Yes, I have heard."

"I haven't been, and I won't be. If that has to be part of the wedding ceremony or anything before or after the marriage, the whole thing is off."

Jeidid sat a time, then he nodded. "You were married in Hedaidile's village without such procedure?"

"Of course."

"There is, then ... how do you say it... a precedent?"

"That's one way to put it."

Jeidid smiled. "I will use that precedent as an argument with my elders. I will let you know in a day or perhaps two what they decide."

Over protests, apparently from Ulana and perhaps others, Jeidid did get the agreement from the elders that no mutilating ritual would be performed. And Leslie, her conditions met, or promised, stepped, for the second time in less than a year, toward the tradition-laden world of Rendille matrimony.

Deelia and the other women helped Leslie build her own dwelling, a bright, clean structure of the same design as all the others in the village. Leslie would move in the day of the wedding.

On the afternoon of the day before the event, she sat with Eric in her arms and Deelia at her side and watched the positioning of tree branches beside the entrance to Deelia's dwelling. Deciduous of some kind, the boughs were brought down from the mountain to make the ceremonial arch. Without a mother to provide the home for the exchanging of vows, the hut of Leslie's hostess would have to suffice.

Preparatory events had already started in the village. Symbolic exchanges of camels and goats had been taking place for two days. Men drove animals in and out of the corral, and at various times, broke into sessions of shouting and jumping. As part of the ritual, Jeidid and his best man, an elder named Jeisel, had given their sandals to Deelia.

As Leslie's designated sponsor Deelia was required to keep the footware until the day of the wedding—an insurance policy—certainly not needed in this case—against the bridegroom running off before the nuptials. Both men now walked about the village barefoot.

"This morning Jeidid has killed a bullock for the wedding feast," said Deelia. She sniffed the air. "Already I can smell the roasting of it in the courtyard. Married women and elders will, tomorrow, enjoy the eating that Jeidid makes ready for them."

"There was a similar feast when Firingin and I were married," said Leslie.

Deelia spoke in a whisper. "It would be better, Less lee, if you did not speak of your last marriage. Many women in the village are unhappy with Jeidid because he chose you to be one of his wives. It is only his power and his generosity that has allowed him to overcome their criticism."

Leslie nodded, not surprised at disagreement from Ulana and others like her.

Deelia quickly added, "But, I am not one who criticizes. I am pleased that Jeidid is so happy."

"He's happy because he'll soon have his long- sought heir," replied Leslie.

Deelia looked toward the horizon. "Jeidid will have many heirs. I am sure of it."

Leslie humored her companion. "It's possible, I suppose."

Deelia smiled. "Next time he comes to me, I know I'll be ready and will then give him a new son."

"Perhaps," said Leslie, smiling to herself. An unbelievable giddiness then came over her. Imagine sitting and talking with a woman who shared your husband about her sex with him. She stifled her impulse to laugh or perhaps it was to cry.

The following morning, Leslie dressed in a goatskin wedding gown and put on the traditional necklace and ear chains. Deelia fussed over every detail of the attire—she'd been working for days, taking in the garment—it had last been used at the wedding of Jeidid and his fourth wife, a large woman named Hedila.

Shortly after the sun passed the high-noon point, Jeidid and Jeisel appeared at the doorway. The saying of vows would be done inside the decorated dwelling. With a senior elder named Jesu conducting the affair, utterances were made in a ritualistic dialect not familiar to Leslie. She nodded and looked submissive when prompted by Deelia, and then with Leslie carrying Eric, the entire wedding party marched under the leafy arch and out of the village for the traditional trek in the desert. At sunset, after several hours of parading, men in front and women following, the group returned to the courtyard. The feasting and celebrating was already underway, but Leslie, feeling some of the old soreness in her feet, begged to be excused.

Jeidid looked disappointed and asked her to stay. She consented to join him in one circle of dancing, and after finishing the set, made her way to the newly furnished dwelling.

She sat in the fresh smelling interior, listening to sounds of the continuing celebration, and suddenly, it all seemed like a dream, an existence that just wasn't real, a life that could be gone in the blink of an eye. She shook off the thought and prepared her bedmat for sleep.

She fed Eric and was about to drift off when a thump at the doorway made her sit upright.

In the shadows, she could see Jeidid, leaning against the sides of the opening. His wedding garment was stained and a sleeve was torn lose from the shoulder stitching. His breath reeked with the odor of rancid mash and milk.

She said nothing.

He attempted to stand and banged his head on the ceiling.

He spoke in Rendille, a curse perhaps. Then he stared at her. In slurred English, he said, "I smell like a sheep, I suppose."

She nodded. "Or worse."

He moved toward her. By the moonlight coming through the smoke hole, she saw him hold out a small vessel.

She recoiled. "No I don't want anything to drink."

"It's oil for scenting our bodies."

He pulled the stopper and poured a liquid into his open palm. He held the hand toward her. "Want to smell?"

She sniffed. It wasn't bad.

"It's from Gof," said Jeidid. "Something he made for us."

She poured from the vessel and rubbed the mixture on her arm.

Jeidid sat by the fireplace. After a time, he removed his hat and started to loosen his wrap.

He stopped.

"No that's backwards," he said. "In America the men undress the women, don't they?"

She felt herself grinning. "Sometimes, I guess."

Under the folds of his clothing, Jeidid rubbed quantities of oil on himself. The scent seemed to overpower the odor from his drinking.

Leslie sat watching him and felt the stirring of a long-neglected desire.

Jeidid undressed her and unlike Firingin, voluntarily came to her in the missionary position. His touch was so tender she almost cried.

Indeed a strong lover, he held her close and moved his body slowly and deliberately. When she started to climax, he thrust frantically. She felt herself clutching at him.

In time, they both pulled back and breathing hard, rested in each others arms.

From what she'd seen during her vigils outside Deelia's dwelling, she expected this husband to now get up, dress himself and leave.

He didn't.

In the darkness, he came to her again and again. Not until sunrise did he move away from her bedmat and put on his clothes.

She offered him some food, dates she'd brought from Deelia's. He sat by the hearth and ate a few.

Before he left, he told her that he would start that day for Marsabit. "Soon you and our son will be registered citizens of Kenya," he said.

After he was gone, she felt a great longing.

Eight days later, Leslie and Deelia sat in Leslie's dwelling. Leslie tried to interest her young companion in the school they would soon be starting.

"When Jeidid returns," said Leslie, "we will have new notepads and pencils. Then we will form our classes, one together at first and then one for each of us."

Deelia showed no enthusiasm.

A loud shout from the direction of the courtyard, and without hesitation, Deelia crawled away to look outside.

"Everyone is running," she said. "Some toward the courtyard. Others in the opposite direction."

Leslie moved Deelia aside and looked for herself.

It was true, everybody seemed to be running and shouting.

One man ran close to Leslie's doorway. "It is the work of evil spirits," he screamed. "They have made the dead to walk among us!"

"Let's see what this is all about," she said to Deelia, and picking up Eric, made her way toward the tide of running villagers.

The personage of Gof crab walked in the middle of the group.

"Let's follow him," said Leslie. "If there are evil spirits around, I'm sure he'll be the one who finds them."

Deelia made a weak smile.

When Leslie and Deelia reached the plaza, they could see what had caused the commotion. In the center of the open area stood six ragged men and eight dusty camels. With shreaded clumps of hair and loose skin over their bone-pointed bodies, animals and men looked as if they were death itself.

Leslie reasoned that the ghosts were a desert caravan, near starvation and desperate for help. The drivers stood, huddled together, some with their backs to the assembled people.

Gof now gyrated around the bedraggled group, throwing his bones and animal skins.

Some of the people threw rocks at the newcomers.

Deelia reached down for a nearby stone, and Leslie stopped her. "Don't," she said. Deelia looked disappointed.

The tallest of the strangers turned away from the others and looked toward the crowd. His mouth moved but his words were too weak to be heard.

Leslie saw a familiar contour in the man's face.

"Firingin?" She spoke the name as a question and grabbed Deelia's shoulder for support.

"That's my husband," she whispered to Deelia. "My God, what's he doing here? He's supposed to be..."

"Dead," finished Deelia. "Cousin Kaido, he also stands among the ghosts. And Karsi. And Hedad. They are all dead."

Leslie moved toward Firingin. People stood aside and stared.

"Where did you come from?"

No answer. Only a wild stare from his eyes.

"Why don't you sit down?" she added.

"You are real?"

His voice came low and croaking.

"Of course, but why do you ask such a thing?"

"I cannot be sure of what I see. Many days, we have been haunted by phantoms that appeared in our minds. Even now, in this village, we cannot believe the terror we see."

"I can't believe people would be throwing things at you. They are terrified, I guess."

Still acting confused, Firingin surveyed the crowd as if looking for somebody. People now looked toward Leslie and Firingin. The rock throwing had stopped.

Leslie opened the fold of her wrap and held Eric up to him. "Here's your son. He's more than a month old, now."

Firingin looked down at the bundle. Slowly, his face formed a grin.

"His name is Eric Halstrom Hedaidile..." She'd stopped without saying Jeidid's family name, and she looked away.

"You are unwell?" asked Firingin.

She forced a smile. "I'm fine."

She held up Eric a second time. "Isn't he wonderful?" She raised one of Eric's hands. "Look, all of his fingers. Just as they should be."

Firingin touched the baby on the forehead and nodded.

"We have so much to talk about," she said. "Why don't you come to my..." Again she had to stop. Firingin might know that only wives of elders have dwellings in a Rendille village.

He looked toward the cluster of men and camels. "We have lost Jaisut."

"Jaisut? I don't understand."

"Jaisut saved us. He saved us, but we have lost him. We could not find him in the desert. We searched but we had to stop. Our food and water was gone."

"He was from here?"

Firingin frowned.

"This is the salt caravan you left with?"

He shook his head.

She waited.

"Only some of it," he said in a weak voice. "Many camels and boys are gone. The boys were killed by the Turkana."

"The Turkana. Yes, we heard they had killed all of you."

Firingin seemed not to hear.

"Two warriors are with me from Jeiso's village."

"You have been to Jeiso's village?"

Firingin nodded.

She was about to ask him to explain, but he held up a hand to stop her. "I must speak to the headman." He looked around, not moving but obviously examining faces. He looked back to Leslie.

"I do not see the one they call Jeidid."

She said nothing.

"The spirit man thinks we are ghosts. Is the headman of this village hiding?"

"Jeidid is not hiding," she blurted. "He's gone."

Firingin stared at her.

Feeling guilt, she looked away.

"The headman is on a safari?" asked Firingin.

She did not answer.

"You say he is gone. Is he..."

"He's away to Marsabit."

Firingin turned away from her. "I must tell this news of the headman to Karsi. He will want to know of it."

Exhaustion of too many days in the desert had taken away all feelings of joy. Even the drivers who lived in Kulal Village expressed no emotion when Firingin led the column into the settlement.

On its way to the central plaza, the line of men and camels passed people running and screaming. It seemed that terror gripped everyone. The spirit man, the one named Gof, came chanting and throwing things. He followed the caravan, and the people followed behind him. All seemed fearful.

Once in the courtyard, Firingin commanded the camels to a halt. The men of the caravan huddled together. The world of unreality they had seen or imagined for days in the desert had now become a place populated by people throwing taunts and pelting stones. Firingin saw Leslie in the crowd. She leaned against a woman Firingin did not know.

Leslie walked toward him.

His voice faltered when he tried to speak—seized by long breathing of hot desert air.

Leslie talked. His fears that she might be a vision were dispelled by the sound of her voice. She was real.

Firingin looked for the headman of the village.

Leslie showed him the face of their child—a boy child. His son, but it had a strange name.

He looked a time at the baby. He felt pride.

Leslie wanted to talk of things, but Firingin's thoughts were on his caravan and its needs. He asked Leslie about Jeidid.

He believed the headman would stop the curses and the threats, that his generosity would also bring food and water for the drivers and the beasts.

Leslie seemed ashamed by mention of the village elder's name. Firingin thought that strange but said nothing of it. He remembered about the strangeness of Leslie's ways. Presently she told him that the headman was away to Marsabit. It was news he would tell to his group. Perhaps Karsi, the young elder, would have mind to know another who might help.

Confronted by the question, Karsi showed eyes glazed by bewilderment. Firingin turned to the boy-drivers. "Who, here, acts as headman when Jeidid is gone?"

Hedad answered, "My father is that man. He stands there, close behind Gof."

"Your father's name?"

"Jesu. My father is Jesu."

Firingin walked to the one named Jesu. He spit greetings at the man.

Jesu shrunk from him.

"We are not ghosts," said Firingin. "We are from your own caravan. We have brought six of your beasts and much Kenyan money."

Firingin motioned to Karsi.

Still in a trance, the young man shuffled forward.

Firingin held Karsi's arm and spoke to Jesu. "This one, Karsi Wambile, was your caravan leader. You must know him."

Jesu squinted hard at Karsi but remained fearful.

"This one from your village has the shillings paid to the Kulal people for the sale of salt and for use of your beasts by my grandfather."

Jesu said nothing.

Firingin motioned for Karsi to produce the money.

A stream of drool flowed from the young man's mouth, and he made no move. Firingin reached into a pocket of Karsi's robe, withdrew the bills and handed them to Jesu.

Jesu examined the pieces of paper, and his face opened to a grin. He turned to the populace and spoke with a loud voice. "These are not ghosts. They are the ones we thought killed by the Turkana, and they have returned to us. They are alive!"

The assembled people murmured and some moved forward. Jesu held up a hand to hold back the crowd and then held up the shillings. "These from our salt caravan have brought wealth to our village, Kenyan money."

Gof stopped his dancing. He stood a moment then slunk toward the dwellings.

A woman came to Kaido. She appeared to weep. Kaido wept also.

Karsi stumbled toward the camels. A man and a woman ran to him.

Jesu looked at Hedad who stood at Firingin's side and spat a greeting on the boy.

Hedad then wept.

"Why do you weep?" asked Jesu. "Are you not happy to be here?"

"I weep for those who are not here: the warrior and the four drivers who died at the hands of the Turkana; Jaisut who was lost in the storm."

Jesu surveyed the haggard group. "It is true, many are missing." The elder looked toward the sky and appeared to mouth silent words.

After a time, he looked at Firingin. "You are Hedaidile, the one who left here to go to the police, but there are two others with you. They are not known to me."

"They are warriors from my grandfather's village. They have no family here but have need of food and water."

Jesu nodded. With stern eyes, he looked upon Firingin. "Why are you here?" he asked. "What has happened that brings you back to us?"

Firingin answered only of the needs of the caravan. "We have been long in the sun and the wind. Our beasts are weak from traveling without forage or water. Drivers and warriors are in need of food and drink, and places where they may rest."

Jesu regarded the villagers crowding around Karsi and Kaido. He nodded at Hedad who was leaving with the woman who was probably his mother. "It seems that all from here have found their families. You and Hedaidile's warriors will be given shelter and nourishment, but first, I must hear your story."

Firingin made a quick response. "After the Turkana attack, we went to my grandfather's village to seek aid for Karsi who was wounded. When we reached the village of Hedaidile, we found my grandfather there. I did not need to go to the police to free him."

Jesu had another question. "Months have passed since we heard you were all killed. Why did you not return sooner?"

Firingin shook his head and started to walk toward the camels. "We may talk of this later. Give food and drink to Jeiso's warriors. I will stable the beasts and go to my woman."

Jesu stared with eyes that showed great concern.

"You speak of going to the white female?"

Firingin nodded. "Yes, she stands with the crowd, waiting for me."

"I saw you speak to her, before" said Jesu, "but you cannot go to that woman again."

Stunned by the words, Firingin let his eyes dwell on the face of the elder. "She is here. I see her standing. Why can I not return to her?"

"It is not lawful for you to do so."

"Not lawful? By what right will you keep me from her? She is my wife. She holds my son in her arms."

"It is by the right of marriage," said Jesu. "The woman called Leslie is married as the fifth wife of our head elder, the man known as Jeidid Wambile. The child the woman carries in her arms will soon be Jeidid's son by adoption. The marriage was made less than a round moon ago. Jeidid now goes to Marsabit to register the event and to record the adoption of the boy."

Firingin looked upon Leslie. She turned away, and he knew by that and by the strangeness she showed before that Jesu's words were true.

He felt his anger grow.

"I will trade my two beasts for two that are fresh," he said to Jesu, "and I will pay you two more from my herd when I return to Hedaidile's village."

A look of alarm came over Jesu. "You are a man sought by the police for murderous acts, and I can see, by the hatred in your eyes, that you now wish to pursue our honorable leader with evil intent. I will not trade beasts to you."

Firingin's anger erupted. "That village leader is not honorable. He steals women from their rightful husbands. He brings disgrace to all clans of the Rendille people."

"There has been no disgraceful act by our headman. We all believed you were dead. Your woman, as far as Jeidid or anyone else knew, was free to be taken in marriage, and her son had no living father. Every person in this village believed that including the woman you say was stolen. No, you cannot have fresh beasts from our corral."

Firingin stared a time at Jesu then turned away and marched toward the pitiful camels he'd brought from the desert.

Leslie and Deelia stood with the crowd of villagers and watched. Firingin took money from one of the drivers and handed it to Jesu, a senior elder that Leslie recognized; he'd officiated at her wedding with Jeidid. Jesu counted through the bills, and then, in loud voice, announced what she already knew, that the visitors were survivors from the salt caravan. Talking erupted among people in the crowd, and Gof ended his dance and retreated to the shadows. Some people talked to the ragged ones. Jesu talked to Firingin. Because of the crowd, Leslie couldn't get close enough to hear the words. Firingin started to walk away, toward the camels. Jesu said something that made him stop and turn around. The two men appeared to argue. Firingin looked at Leslie, but she could not face his eyes.

She turned her head to Deelia. "I think Jesu has just told Firingin about me and Jeidid."

Deelia nodded.

"What can I say to him?" pleaded Leslie.

"You can say nothing to him. The one you call Firingin is Rendille. He will not talk to a woman about his anger."

"That's crazy! I'm his wife."

Deelia shrugged.

Firingin and the elder seemed ready to fight. "I must stop this," said Leslie. She wrapped both arms around Eric and started to push her way past the people.

Deelia grabbed her. "You will only make it worse."

Leslie jerked away but then saw Firingin turn his back on Jesu and once again, walk toward the camels.

Without a look, he lead a pair of the poor creatures away and out of the courtyard.

She yelled at him.

He paid no attention.

"Where is he going?" she asked no one in particular.

She ran after him, but his angry pace was too fast. She followed to the edge of the village and then watched as Firingin and the camels disappeared behind a nearby hill. Beyond the hill stretched the open desert.

Tears streamed down her cheeks. After a time, Deelia came to stand at her side.

"He's gone, Deelia."

Deelia nodded. "We should now return to our dwellings."

"Return to our dwellings? How can you be so callous? Don't you realize that I've just watched my husband, a man starved for food and delirious from lack of water walk into that glaring inferno. He's going to die out there."

"Whether he lives or dies, that man is no longer your husband."

The comment stunned Leslie. She said nothing for a moment.

She hefted Eric to a more comfortable position on her hip then spoke as if to herself. "The marriage to Jeidid was a mistake. Though everybody said that Firingin was dead, I should have known better. I should never have agreed to any wedding."

"That makes no difference now," replied Deelia. "When Jeidid completes the registration in Marsabit, even the government will say that you are a wife to our head elder. No one, anywhere, will recognize your marriage to the man called Firingin."

Leslie waved her companion away. "I'm going to find out exactly what Jesu said to make him run off like that."

"You can't ask questions of Jesu. He is a senior man in this village."

Leaving Deelia standing, Leslie marched toward the center of the settlement. She stopped at her own dwelling long enough to change Eric's thoroughly-soaked diaper, then she went on to the courtyard.

Most of the people had left. The camels from the caravan were gone, and only two of the ragged men remained. They sat eating in the shade of a palm tree in the center of the opening.

Leslie looked for Jesu, but he was not to be seen.

Desperate for someone to ask about Firingin, she walked toward the two men. Bending low over their portions of food, they did not look up at her. She stopped a distance away from them, the smell of their clothes and bodies made her reluctant to move closer.

Both of the men wore wraps that showed red through heavy layers of dirt. They appeared to be warriors possibly the two from Jeiso's village. Welts and running sores on their decimated bodies attracted a swarm of aggressive flies.

Leslie pulled an extra fold of cloth over Eric's face.

The men wiped their bowls clean with their fingers, and one after the other, they slurped water from a large gourd. They seemed to be finished with their meal.

"Are you from this village?" asked Leslie.

The men looked at her for the first time, then the nearest took another draw on the water. He wiped his mouth.

"I know you," he said. "You are the white woman who taught school for our children. My brother went to your classes."

She smiled. "Yes, I taught school in the village of Jeiso Hedaidile. And you must be from there?"

"We are. It is our home."

"My husband is Firingin. He is Jeiso's grandson."

Both warriors smiled.

The warrior who had talked before said, "We came to help the man, Firingin, bring you back to our village."

The other added, "The old one ordered us to be guards against the Turkana."

"Jeiso?"

The warrior's answer showed surprise at the question. "Yes," he said, "Jeiso is the leader of our family. That you must know already."

"I do know that, but I thought he went to jail."

The warrior took another wipe at his bowl.

Leslie waited.

"The police took him," said the warrior, "but they brought him back."

"Well, that's certainly no surprise to me."

Her last was in English. The warriors did not respond.

The talkative warrior asked if she would bring more food. She said she would try.

The empty bowls clattered into her free hand, and she stood, looking for the person who might have brought the initial serving. A woman near one of the dwellings stirred a large pot over an open fire.

After bringing second helpings to the warriors, Leslie found herself obliged to sit in their odorous presence while they wolfed down the new portions.

Again, they slurped from the jug of water. She watched and when she thought they were finished, she asked, "Firingin left this place with two camels. Do you know where he is going?"

The warriors looked at each other. The bold one answered. "It is said that he goes to a place called Marsabit. It is said that he is very angry."

"At me, I suppose."

The bold warrior answered again. "I do not believe he is angry with you. His anger is against the headman of this village. He goes to Marsabit, we were told, to stop that one from stealing wives."

The emaciated young man clamored to his feet and looked grimly toward the eastern horizon.

"The man Firingin goes, but he will not reach Marsabit. We have just come from the desert he wishes to cross. It is hotter than any near our village. He has no food and no water and there is none on the camels. He will die. His camels will die, also."

"Why don't you follow him? He will not move fast. You could bring him back to this place. I could talk to..."

The warrior shook his head. "He would not listen to us. We are only boys to him. He has hate that is powerful. He will go fast until he can go no more."

Leslie looked away and said nothing.

Firingin tugged the stumbling camels across the low hills east of the village and then onto the broad flatlands of the desert. Fueled by raging fury, his legs churned onward for nearly an hour then slowed to a wobbly stagger.

The muscles of his body tightened with pain. His lungs ached, and a dryness deep in his throat rasped with each breath he took. A weakness grew in his body. His knees buckled, and he fell. The camels shuffled a few steps farther, then without a command, they both kneeled.

Firingin crawled on hands and knees to a patch of shade made by the older beast. He crouched beside her and stared at the terrain with blank eyes. Flat and searing, it stretched before him. Uncounted pebbles covered the sandy soil. Occasionally a rise of hardened ground showed, bare and dark in the continuum. Balls of thorns tumbled in the light breeze.

In his half-conscious condition, Firingin fumbled in the supply carrier on the old camel's back.

All the food containers and water bottles were empty. He would have known that, but his mind was not thinking at the level of knowing things.

He ran a finger inside the rim of a water flask and brought back the green powder of evaporated scum. He licked the finger and tasted the bitterness. He spit or tried to.

He rummaged deeper into the pack, looking for any morsel of grain or container of liquid that might have been overlooked during those frantic days when the caravan searched for Jaisut. He found bags holding shredded remains of the caravan's tents—nothing he could eat or drink. Under the bags, wrapped in a skin, he found a coil of rope, a shovel, a hammer and several steel stakes. The two rifles the warriors had stopped carrying glistened beside the wrapping.

Firingin worked to the other side of the camel and pawed through a tattered sack containing cooking pots, stones for grinding millet, and knives and spoons. An oilcloth tied to the frame contained rawhide lengths, a bow and a pair of arrows for bleeding camels.

No bleeding had been done on the caravan, and leaning back against the side of old camel, Firingin wondered if it would be possible for him, alone in this open desert, to do such a thing.

His second camel, a young bull, could probably survive the loss of blood, but how might the operation be accomplished?

He remembered the bleeding in the ravine and cast eyes about, looking for ground that might hold the needed restraints. A few meters away, a rise of firm, darkened soil presented itself, and feeling a rush of excitement, Firingin unpacked the coil of rope, the hammer, and three of the stakes. He clamored to his feet, and using all of the determination he could muster, he drove the stakes into the knoll of hardened ground, two close together and one apart. He then went back to the camels and commanded them to stand.

The old one obeyed, but the bull stayed down.

Firingin commanded again, using the pry of a foot under the flattened belly, and the young beast stiffly rose to its feet. Firingin led both animals to the protruding stakes. He tied the lead rope of the old camel to the stake by itself. The bull's halter he secured to one of the pair together. He hobbled the creature and tethered a length of the rope between the hind legs and the third stake. He then shoved hard with his shoulders until the bull-camel fell.

Working as fast as he could, Firingin tied a rawhide thong around the extended neck, and when the jugular bulged with blocked blood, he fired one of the arrows. Two flasks filled, and Firingin released the tourniquet. He then poured some of the blood on the ground and stirred to make a slurry. He slapped the mud over the wound and bound it tight, using cloth torn from a fold of his robe. He released the hobbles and the tether, and prayed that the animal would rise.

It did not. Motionless it laid as if dead.

Firingin prodded with a tip of the bow.

The camel rolled an eye but gave no further response.

Firingin shouted.

The legs of the beast flailed, and Firingin prodded again and shouted louder. The creature struggled to its feet but fell back.

Firingin feared the camel would die. He would give it no more commands. The bull lay for a time, and then, as if embarrassed by its weakness, the animal pushed hard with its front legs, and levered itself to stand.

Firingin patted the face and spoke soothing words. He then drank both containers of the bull's blood. He drank the nourishment, tepid and salty, and he felt the flow of energy into his body.

No longer blinded by anger, he thought of Jeidid. That man will not know of my pursuit, he reasoned. He will not feel the need for speed. If I make haste, I may find him before he talks to those who would do the registrations. Firingin remembered the wise ways of the Kulal headman. A hard trader of camels, but Jeidid was not evil. When he sees that I am not dead, he will not keep Leslie, and he will not take my son.

Firingin untied both camels and pulled up the stakes. He stowed the equipment and commanded the beasts forward.

The animals moved a few steps then stopped.

Firingin strained on the lead rope. The camels walked but showed no strength for hurrying.

He tried to think of a place where he could find water and forage for the beasts and remembered the oasis near the ravine. It would not be far south of the route he wished to take. He would lose a day, but his camels would be refreshed and he would make up the time.

He turned, putting the afternoon sun above his right shoulder, and urged his animals into a slow gate.

Leslie sat in her dwelling and cried. Seeing Firingin again, emaciated and wanting, had kindled all the old feelings, her deep love and her strong desire to be with him. If only she'd said right away that she and Jeidid had been married... Firingin might have listened then. She could have told him how she'd believed he was dead, how she'd been convinced that she couldn't have kept the baby. She could have told Firingin that she would demand to have the wedding annulled.

Throughout the afternoon she wept her tears of despair, and by the evening, she could cry no more. She fed Eric and choked down a meal of dry bread and dates. After eating, she crawled outside where the air was cooler. She sat with her child, by her doorway, and thought of her future.

"Jeidid will soon return with everything all signed and recorded," she muttered to herself. "Firingin will be dead, and I'll be Jeidid's number five wife forever."

The prospect now made her shiver.

Eric, roused by the motion, nuzzled close for another meal. She put him to her breast.

"Still I do like Jeidid," she said with a quiet voice. "Handsome, intelligent and seemingly considerate... who wouldn't like such a man? But love him? How can you love someone you hardly know?"

She remembered the night of their wedding. He'd been so tender.

A smile played at her lips—a smile that soon faded against her feeling of guilt.

Tears again. She shook them off. I'll soon have my school, she thought. But not like the one at Jeiso's village. The mothers here can't be expected to help that way and bring meals. They're just not as friendly as they were in Jeiso's community.... I'd go back there in a minute, if I could...

The following morning Deelia appeared at the doorway of Leslie's dwelling. She placed a container of milk and a bag of cracked millet on Leslie's hearth.

"For your meals today."

Leslie thanked her.

Deelia said nothing for a moment, then asked if Leslie would be going to the morning circle.

Leslie bristled at the question. She poked at the dead coals in her fireplace and hoped that Deelia would go away.

Deelia did not. "That man, Firingin, will not be back," she said. "You must forget about him. Come. The women at the circle will help you forget."

Leslie glared her resentment. "You don't understand, do you? I'm not sad just because of Firingin. I'm sad, as much as anything, because of the mess I've made... the trouble and suffering I've brought to so many people I care about... Firingin for sure, but also for my friends and my baby."

"Trouble?" asked Deelia. "Suffering?... Caused by you? You are correct. I do not understand this sadness you feel."

Leslie attempted an explanation. "It's like this. If I had gone back when the police first came to Jeiso's village, I could have told them that Firingin was trying to return me to the tour group and was attacked by the soldier. I could have told them that he'd killed that man in self-defense."

Deelia looked puzzled.

"The helicopter raids never would have happened--except for the first one. Firingin wouldn't have had to go back to free Jeiso. In fact, he wouldn't have even had to leave Jeiso's village... Well, maybe for the trial, but that wouldn't have lasted long, once I'd given my testimony."

"But you would have been gone," said Deelia. "The police wouldn't have let you come back."

"That's probably true, but the Kenyans wouldn't have known I was pregnant. I could have gone with my baby inside me, and nobody would have known."

Deelia appeared to be taken aback. "Others would have been hurt by you going away. I would never have known you and your baby and would have missed the happiness you have brought to me."

Leslie studied the sad, young face before her. After a time, she smiled a weak smile. "You go on to the circle, by yourself, Deelia. Maybe tomorrow I'll come."

Deelia shook her head. "I will not go there this morning. When I have finished my chores, I will come back here. Then we can work together, making ready for the school we will start."

Stunned by the words, Leslie stared in disbelief.

"But you don't..."

"I will do it because of you. Because we are friends, yes. And because our husband wants this school."

Later, with Deelia at her side, Leslie sorted through the bundle of classroom supplies she had brought from Jeiso's village. Using cooking knives, she and Deelia sharpened the pencils to needle points. Marks on used pieces of paper were erased, and the sheets carefully pressed between selected pairs of flat rocks. Notes made while Leslie taught at Jeiso's community were reviewed. They would provided rough lesson plans for the new classes.

"Tomorrow we will start the visits to the dwellings of village mothers," said Leslie.

Deelia smiled. "See, already you are over your sadness."

"I will always be sad about the things that have happened. But you're right. I am feeling better, now that I'm busy."

Deelia nodded, and Leslie returned to the work at hand. "Perhaps you can help me make a list of those mothers who have school-aged girls and boys."

Deelia frowned. "Girls cannot come to school. The elders and many of the women would object if we have other than boys as our students."

"Yes, it was that way at Jeiso's at first. But, I thought since you went to school..."

"I did go, but it was to a government school. The people in my village could not say no when the Kenyans ordered girls to be sent."

"Okay, then. We'll only go to the mothers of boys. Later, we'll try to bring in the girls."

Deelia said nothing.

"During the visits," explained Leslie, "we will describe the school project and will inform each mother that Jeidid approves and gives it full support. Then we will try to get the names and ages of the boys who will attend."

The following day, when they went out with the message, they found that many women were afraid. Leslie, with Deelia's help, tried to tell those mothers of the benefits, the value of learning numbers and reading and also the fact that the school would be a place where energetic sons would be away for the several hours of each day's classes.

Many of the women were swayed by the second benefit, and a few welcomed the chance for their children to learn without having to leave the village. One young mother talked of dreams she had for her son. She mixed English words with her Rendille as she spoke of him going, some day, to the great university in the Kenyan city of Nairobi.

That evening, after Eric nursed, he laid on the bedmat, smiling his toothless smiles at Leslie. She put him on his belly. He giggled, and she noticed, as she had many times in the past, that his eyes showed the same sparkle as Firingin's.

She fought sadness and then thought of Firingin's anger and savage reaction after hearing about the marriage.

She shook her head. It had always been that way with Firingin. He would never wait to discuss things. Brave to a fault and strong, but he would not talk, and he would never listen.

Crying tears of anger and remorse, Leslie curled up beside Eric and tried to sleep.

After chores and women's circle the following morning, Deelia and Leslie sat by the doorway of Leslie's dwelling and prepared for the day's visits.

"Ulana's sister has two young sons," offered Deelia. "We should be sure and go to her."

"I hope she's more receptive than Ulana."

"She is. Ulana is the eldest and the most traditional woman in her family."

Leslie nodded. "Any others with more than one son?"

Deelia recited the names, and Leslie added them to the list.

"I better change Eric and feed him," said Leslie. "Then we can be on our way."

She crawled with the baby into the dwelling, and while Eric ravenously snorted at his morning meal, she fumbled in the pile of clothing for a clean diaper.

From outside Deelia asked if Leslie thought Jeidid would be back before the day was over.

"He's only been gone ten days," answered Leslie. "It must take longer than that for a trip to Marsabit."

"He has fast camels. The warriors with him are good runners."

Leslie, tying the fresh diaper on the baby, said nothing.

Suddenly Deelia let out an ear-piercing scream. "Jeidid has been killed!" she wailed. "I know it. Our husband is murdered!"

The outburst frightened Eric. "Deelia, stop it!"

Hurrying out of the dwelling, Leslie found her helpmate bent over at the waist and sobbing.

Shaking the young woman by a shoulder, Leslie shouted, "Deelia, what's gotten into you? Jeidid isn't dead. His caravan traveled east, and the Turkana are no longer active in that direction."

Deelia looked up, still weeping.

Leslie shifted Eric to her hip and wrapped her free arm around Deelia. "He'll be back. It takes time to do things with people from the government."

Deelia managed a tentative smile.

Both women sat silent.

Leslie had spoken words of consolation, but inside she wondered. What images had Deelia seen that frightened her so?

Rendille people often showed strong connections to the natural, and also the supernatural. Leslie had seen indications in the past: awareness of changes in the weather days before anything happened; sensitivity to the moods of camels and other livestock; auras of joy or gloom that inexplicably swept through the community. Could it be that an ethereal message about Jeidid had somehow come to Deelia?

She thought about it a moment.

"That's crazy," she said to herself.

33

Firingin stopped for rest at least a dozen times during the westward passage. Each time, the animals kneeled, and he hunkered beside their heads, clucking reassurances until their breathing slowed toward normal. Near sunset, he and his exhausted beasts reached the tribal trail and turned south. A short time later, the bull-camel dropped to its knees, panting, and though the interval had been short since the last stop, Firingin waited for the animal to recover. When the creature seemed normal, he gave the command to rise, but the bull did not obey. Fixed to the ground by fatigue or by obstinateness, the beast would not make the effort, and seeing the sun sinking toward night, Firingin had no patience for pleading. He untied the lead rope and let the young animal lie. He would continue to the oasis with the she-camel and come back later for the bull.

The evening winds had started, and Firingin stopped in the lee of a small hill. He did not make camp but laid his body in the open beside the resting she-camel.

He wondered if he would find high, uncropped grass at the oasis. The tribal trail had shown little evidence of traffic. Turkana terror had kept travelers away, and many places blowing sand had obscured the pathway.

Exhausted, Firingin fell asleep quickly and did not wake until his face felt the warmth of sun upon it. Angry about the time lost by his extended slumber, he shot to his feet and prodded the camel to life.

The sun had climbed high overhead by the time the pair reached the hill overlooking the oasis.

Firingin surveyed the scene below.

No sign of humans or animals. Palms near the watering hole swayed, scraggly as before, but a greenish hue over the ground promised fresh grass and a clear flow of water.

The camel smelled the moisture, and Firingin let her run. He followed behind, knowing that she would go no farther than the drinking and the grazing.

He reached the campground and felt nostalgia for the times he had been there with Leslie. He stood facing north and mouthed a vow to be with her again. He drank great gulps from the spring and set to work. He harvested bundles of grass and tied them on the camel's carrier along with bottles filled with fresh water.

Before darkness, Firingin and the she-camel left the oasis. They moved northward, and when the strong winds came, they kept going. After midnight, they reached the place where the bull-camel had collapsed. There was no sign of the animal. Firingin saw him nowhere—not as a heap on the ground nor up and meandering over nearby knolls.

Firingin made a clucking call into the silence.

No reply.

He walked off the trail, leading the she-camel, and saw nothing of the younger beast. Perhaps a whiff from the distant spring had lured the bull toward the oasis.

Firingin moved south again and on the trail saw signs of intruders, fresh footprints of camels and drivers. He noted the place where the travelers had intercepted the pathway. Four men had come from the direction of the Chalbi with a caravan of two camels.

One of the animals dragged its hind leg—injured. Firingin thought of Turkana, but did not believe they would have patience to travel with a crippled camel.

In late morning, Firingin and the she-camel arrived, the second time in two days, at the low hill above the oasis. He tethered the animal behind a rise in the ground and crawled forward.

He did not see the bull, but a two-camel caravan camped near the palm grove. Tents showed that some of the travelers were resting. Two men stood guard. They wore the red wraps of Rendille warriors.

Firingin and his beast descended into the basin. He did not know the sentries but expected them to be friendly. Rendille always gave welcome to fellow tribesmen.

The warriors saw him and moved their rifles to a ready position.

Firingin held up a hand in greeting.

A third warrior came from one of the tents. A man dressed as an elder emerged from another.

When he saw the elder's face, Firingin let out a whoop. The elder was the man he sought, Jeidid!

Jeidid rubbed at his eyes and stared.

Firingin walked toward him.

Jeidid's face showed apprehension.

He does not know me, thought Firingin. I appear much poorer in body than when he last saw me. My robe is torn and soiled from the long trip.

Firingin spoke, using Jeidid's name.

Jeidid spoke to the sentries, and they lowered their weapons.

"I am Hedaidile," said Firingin. "The one who left your village to go to the police."

"I know who you are," answered Jeidid, "But what are you doing here? We heard all on the salt-caravan were killed by the Turkana."

"Some of us escaped."

Jeidid's eyes looked in the direction of Firingin's approach. "But you travel alone?"

Firingin nodded. "The others are at your village."

Jeidid looked to the north and said nothing.

"They are with their families," said Firingin, "but I have come away from that place on a mission to find you."

Jeidid did not respond.

Firingin added, "It was said at Kulal that you have married my woman."

Jeidid opened his mouth as if to say something but closed it again.

Firingin waited.

"You need food and water," said Jeidid. "Come eat of our honey and of our millet and dates. Drink of our tea." He gave a sign to one of the warriors. "Prepare a meal for this grandson of Hedaidile."

Firingin smiled.

Jeidid waved a hand toward the firepit. "Eat and drink, then we will talk of your mission."

Pleased at the offer of a cooked meal, Firingin did not object to the delay.

Jeidid returned to the shade of his tent.

Firingin walked to his camel. He would place hobbles so the beast could graze with freedom.

The warrior preparing the meal, a young man with a cheerful face, smiled. Firingin, smelling the steaming porridge, felt his body tremble. The many days since he'd last eaten a full breakfast made him weak against the odors of cooking.

The warrior handed him a bowl of tea.

Firingin drank it too hot and had to spit it out.

The warrior laughed.

Firingin held the bowl for a second filling.

He felt the warmth as he sipped, and he felt tears of gratitude in his eyes.

After two helpings of millet with honey, he sat back and enjoyed a sweet gurgle in his stomach.

The attending warrior cleaned the bowls. The sentries had

walked to the shade of a palm tree.

Jeidid came out of his tent and stood near Firingin.

"I thank you for your hospitality," said Firingin.

Jeidid nodded. "The least we could do for Jeiso Hedaidile's grandson."

"So, now we will talk?"

Jeidid nodded again. "Now I will learn about the raid on my caravan. You say the others are at the village?"

"Karsi, Hedad and Kaido are at your village. The other boys and both warriors are dead. All but Jaisut were killed by the Turkana. Jaisut was lost in a sandstorm."

Jeidid's eyes showed sadness. He said nothing for a time, then he asked, "The camels? They were all lost?"

"Six survived. They are at Kulal."

Again silence from Jeidid.

Firingin spoke of Jaisut's heroism.

"He was our best shooter," said Jeidid.

"He taught me how to use the shooting weapons," said Firingin.

Jeidid seemed to think on Firingin's words, then asked, "What happened to your plans to free Jeiso? I thought you were going to surrender yourself to the police. Why are you now roaming the deserts, looking for me?"

Firingin sensed hostility in the question and answered with caution. "I am free because the police no longer seek me."

Jeidid's response came with a sneer. "They no longer believe you to be a murderer?"

Firingin did not answer.

"What about your grandfather? Have you left him to sit in a Kenyan prison? Is he now suffering for the things you have done?"

Firingin felt the ridicule of the question but would not let anger show in his answer. "Jeiso is at his home. He was released before I and those from your caravan came to Hedaidile Village. He said the Kenyans found no fault in him, and because of his words to them, they now believe me to be dead... also my woman."

"He has told you these things?"

"I have spoken to him many times. He bought blocks of salt from your caravan. Twenty thousand Kenyan shillings have been paid by him."

Jeidid looked away.

Firingin continued. "Jeiso now waits for my return with Leslie and with his great-grandson, a boy with a strange name, but still my son."

Jeidid remained silent.

"The woman, Leslie, that I left in your care will be greeted with great honor in Hedaidile Village."

Jeidid's eyes hardened. "You cannot honor any woman. You are a criminal, young Hedaidile. No matter what the police believe, you have killed one of their officers. You wish to escape from that crime and wish to disrupt a marriage and an adoption legally recorded by the Kenyan Government. You wish to do these things, but you cannot."

Jeidid put his face to Firingin's and spoke with a angry voice. "You are from an honorable family, but you are not one to be honored. You must pay for your acts. You must be taken away to the police and there you will be judged on the things you have done to them and to your people."

Firingin saw the manipulation in Jeidid's words. They heaped shame that would make some men want crawl away and leave their wives and their children. He shook his head at the elder. "I know of my position. I have wealth and honor in Hedaidile Village. I have status in my family, and I will not be swayed by your words. The woman is mine, and in time, she will be with me."

He stood to go to his camel. He would leave Jeidid and go to the green cavern in the nearby ravine. Eating the flesh of snakes and lizards, he would grow strong again. Soon he would return to his grandfather's village, and with the old one's wisdom to guide him, he would find a way to bring Leslie and the boy to their rightful home.

Jeidid motioned to the young warrior who still washed cooking pots. "This grandson of Hedaidile is a criminal. Seize him!"

The warrior, with water wet on his hands, hesitated, and Firingin ran toward the old camel.

Jeidid yelled to the sentries by the palm tree.

"Shoot him! Shoot him before he gets away!"

Firingin reached under the camel to release the hobble-ropes and heard the first rifle shot crack the air.

A pounding of fear filled Firingin's head. How can this be— shooting coming from my own kinsmen?

He saw the two from the palm tree take positions between the camel and the desert.

Another shot came. Firingin moved behind the camel's body.

A third shot and the old camel squealed with pain. Her knees buckled, and she fell on one side.

Firingin flattened himself beside her head. He saw her eyes cloud with the film of death. She kicked once and laid still. He touched her nose. The breathing had stopped.

He raised his head to look for the sentries. He saw only one. The other must have hidden himself. Jeidid and the warrior who had cooked could not be seen. They were probably at the tents, behind the mound of the camel's stomach.

Firingin removed bags of gear from the high part of the dead camel's carrier. Keeping his body low, he placed them as a barrier between him and the visible sentry.

The two rifles glistened, exposed on the carrier.

A shot from the warrior splintered a brace near the weapons. Keeping his head down, Firingin untied one of the rifles. He moved the bolt to load a bullet.

When he had learned shooting from Jaisut, the killing of jackals had been easy. The noise hurt his ears—nothing more.

Another shot. The shooting had been coming slow. The sentries weapons were the single-shot kind—the same as those carried on the salt caravan. With only one warrior shooting, Firingin might make an escape.

He laid the barrel of his rifle over the dead camel's belly and lifted his head to look for the second sentry. He swung the sights of the weapon in an arc, inspecting the scene.

By the tents, he saw Jeidid and the warrior who'd done the cooking. The warrior had only a spear. Jeidid had no weapon at all.

Jeidid yelled orders to his sentries. He told them to charge Firingin's barricade.

Firingin heard one warrior shout back that he would be killed if he charged. Firingin saw the other warrior sitting by a palm tree, working the bolt of his rifle. The weapon seemed to be jammed. Firingin scanned further and saw the first sentry kneeling for a shot.

Firingin heard the report and saw a fresh furrow open in the old camel's flank. He pointed his rifle at the warrior who worked on the jammed bullet.

That one must have seen the glint of the moving barrel. He jumped to his feet and ran, screaming, toward the tents.

Firingin tracked him with the sights but did not shoot. He thought of Jaisut, another who had worn the red of Rendille warriors.

A bullet rang a pot in the bag of cooking gear.

Firingin would go after the next shot.

He laid down and waited for the sound. His muscles tensed. He would jump up and run as soon as he heard the report. He had eaten well at Jeidid's fire. He hoped energy from the food would bring strength to his legs.

He heard Jeidid's voice, angry, from the direction of the tents. The words told of the problem with the rifle. The warrior's answer gave excuses. Without warning, an exploding sound came. Firingin flattened himself on the ground and looked over the camel and toward the tents.

Jeidid's body lay in a heap on the ground, and the sentry who'd run with the rifle looked with horror at a dark wound in the elder's chest. Shattered wood and ribbons of twisted metal distorted the shape of the shooting weapon.

Firingin saw blood gush from Jeidid and spread as a crimson pool on the white robe. Without thinking he stood and stepped over the camel's neck, he must help the fallen leader.

He heard the report from behind. A sting under his right arm-pit made him grab with his left hand.

Warm blood oozed through his fingers.

He pulled back the hand and sat where he stood. A stream of red ran down his side and grew into a mottled stain in the soil.

He looked toward the warrior with the single-shot weapon and saw him fishing in his pouch for another bullet. Firingin pulled himself behind the barricade and panting, he laid beside the hulk of his camel. Wadding up a fold of his robe, he tried to stop the bleed-ing.

No shot came. He elevated his head to see. The sentry who'd been shooting was gone. His weapon laid near the post where he'd been.

Firingin fell back.

Only spears were left. If he could run, he could still get away.

He struggled to rise to his feet. He tasted the millet, and dizzi-ness swam in his head. He saw the sky and the ground move as wheel. He retched, and millet came up.

From a distance greater than it should have been, he heard shout-ing.

He raised his head and saw a camel hopping as a bird and war-riors chasing.

His mouth tasted dry. Under the desert sun, he trembled, and his eyes closed.

34

In the dead of night, Leslie heard the warbling sounds, a cadence she recognized as the Rendille women's mourning chant. She crawled to the doorway of her dwelling and looked into the moonlit village and saw shadows of people running toward the warbling. Some of the runners shouted, and some wailed. Deelia ran by, screaming undecipherable words.

Leslie thought of waking Eric so she could join the runners, but he'd only been asleep for about an hour and wasn't dropping off easily nowadays. She crouched by the opening and watched. Perhaps one of those passing would come near enough so she could get their attention and ask what had happened. Gof slithered by a few feet from her. She spoke to him, but he paid no attention. Then came one of Jeiso's warriors. He looked in her direction, and she motioned for him to approach the dwelling.

"What is going on?" she asked.

He looked toward the hurrying people. "Warriors from this village have come from the south. It is said they have brought their headman's body."

"Oh my God!" She bit her lips. "Jeidid? He's dead?"

The warrior nodded.

"Did Firingin...?"

"I do not know," answered the warrior, impatience showing in his eyes. "I must go and then I will find out."

"Yes, go. Go and learn what has happened and then come and tell me. I have to stay here with my child."

The warrior ran into the darkness, and Leslie sat, reeling from the shock. She'd been prepared for the loss of Firingin. His rabid charge into the desert with no food or water had left little doubt that he would soon be dead. She'd already cried for him, but Jeidid? How could it be that he was gone. Could Firingin, weak as he was, possibly have killed him? She thought of Deelia's premonition. How could the young woman have known?

Leslie looked around the inside of her dwelling. "I'd better pack," she said out loud. "If Firingin did kill Jeidid, Eric and I might have to flee for our lives." The people of Kulal village could blame us for this. Many of them had resented the marriage to Jeidid and would see it as the reason for his death.

Minutes later, Deelia looked in at Leslie's doorway.

"Our husband is dead, Less-lee."

The sound of her voice woke Eric, and Leslie went to comfort him.

Convulsions shook Deelia. Leslie returned and hugged her with the free arm. "I know, Deelia. I'm so sad for all of us."

Deelia sniffed back her tears. "He was shot... His body is all covered with blood..." More spasms of grief.

"Shot?" said Leslie.

Deelia wiped away tears. "The warriors say it was a fight with the one named Firingin. The warriors say there was much shooting."

"But Firingin doesn't have a gun. I don't understand this."

Deelia seemed not to hear. "The warriors say that the one, Firingin, is dead too. They said they left him lying by his dead camel in a pool of his own blood."

"Where? What place did they leave him?"

Deelia shook her head. "At the place of the fight, a spring, a watering hole south of here. Why do you care where he lies?"

"I care because he was my husband, the father of my child. He should not lie alone."

Deelia seemed startled by those words. "But Jeidid was your husband, how can you...?" She stared a moment, and then saying nothing more, she backed out of the dwelling.

Leslie sat dry-eyed, overwhelmed by the barrage of events.

"Why would they fight?" she asked herself. "Jeidid should certainly have known better." She shook her head. "Male superiority. The unwillingness to discuss anything. That's the cause of all this."

Tears finally came. Tears of anger.

Eric had quieted down, and Leslie put him on the bedmat. She dried her eyes and continued to pack.

Presently Jeiso's warrior returned. "I have learned of the death," he said. "It was caused by Firingin. And he is dead also. Left at the place of the fighting." He stopped talking and looked around.

"You are packing? Are you going away from here?"

"Yes, I think I have to. Get your partner and buy a camel for our trip." Realizing her status as the wife of Jeiso's grandson, she felt comfortable giving orders to one of the Hedaidile warriors.

"But I have nothing to pay for a camel," the warrior replied.

Leslie rummaged through a box on her hearth. "Here, take these. They are my wedding jewels. They will be more than enough to buy one camel. Now go and come back here with the animal and the other warrior. We will go to the place where Firingin lies, and we will bury him. Then we will go south to Jeiso's Village."

The ritualistic sounds of mourning continued to fill the air as Leslie climbed aboard the kneeled camel. A nervous-looking warrior held Eric and quickly handed him up after the animal had risen to its feet.

"Go directly out of the village," said Leslie. "There are people I would like to say goodbye to, but I don't want to be seen leaving."

The warrior commanded the camel forward, and the small procession moved silently toward the southbound trail.

Minutes later, the only sounds to be heard came from the scuffing of feet against the dry ground and the occasional grunt of the beast under Leslie.

The rocking motion seemed to relax Eric. He slept, and Leslie thought of the future. I will go to the police soon after we get to Jeiso's Village, she decided. I'll tell them everything. I'll clear Firingin's name, and I'll see about reversing the marriage to Jeidid and the adoption of Eric as his son.

Maybe, I'll ask the Kenyans to send me home. With Firingin's name cleared they will have no reason to keep me or my child, and with Firingin dead, I don't think I'll want to stay in this land. Memories would be too oppressive. Besides, Jeiso and the others may not want me to stay after they hear of all the trouble I've caused.

After a time she asked the warrior who walked beside the camel if he thought that Firingin had killed Jeidid. The warrior, the one who seldom talked, shrugged.

"They say Jeidid was shot. How could Firingin do such a thing?" The warrior shrugged again.

Near noon the following day, the column arrived at the watering hole. From a distance Leslie recognized the site as the place where she and Firingin had decided to go to the nearby hills for a break in their northbound trek. "I've been here before," she said.

The warrior said nothing.

The flaps of two windblown tents fluttered benignly in a gentle breeze, but the rest of the scene showed only chaotic destruction. An injured camel limped on the far side of the spring, obviously frightened by their approach. A bloated carcass lay in the foreground, probably that of Firingin's beast. Bags, cooking pots and other items were piled in disarray on one side of the creature, and pieces of flesh ripped from the animal's neck and hind legs glistened in the sunlight.

Firingin could not be seen; his body was no doubt behind the camel.

Near the tents, a darkened place showed on the ground, the rust color of dried blood. A strangely twisted item that looked like a deformed rifle rested at the edge of the stain.

"What's that?" Leslie asked the warrior.

He ran ahead for a closer look but shied away when he approached the object.

Leslie would have called him back, but a jolt from the camel alerted her to the kneeling that would soon happen. She handed the baby to the warrior-driver.

"Hold him, and I'll try to hang on while this creature does its nose dive."

The warrior smiled and held the child while Leslie managed the maneuver of dismounting.

"I don't see Firingin's body," she said. "Go and look behind the dead camel."

The warrior returned the baby and walked the distance to the reeking hulk.

"He is not here," the warrior shouted back, "Hyenas have taken all of him, I think."

"Oh, Lord."

The warrior scanned a wide circle around the camel. "I see no pieces of him. Perhaps they have dragged him away."

Tears came to Leslie, and she sat heavily on the open ground.

The warrior went to his partner who still stood in rigid vigil over the twisted tangle of steel and wood.

"This was a shooting weapon," the more talkative warrior shouted to Leslie. "But it is blown apart."

Leslie struggled to her feet and walked to join the warriors. Her movements roused Eric from his sleep. He nuzzled for a meal, and she decided to use one of the tents for shade while she fed him.

"Look around for Firingin," she told the warriors and leaned toward the flapped entrance. "He must be..." She let out a scream and backed away from the shelter.

Eric now added a counterpoint to her scream by issuing his own chorus of terrified sounds.

Leslie's voice came husky when she spoke. "He's... in there... "

"Firingin?" asked the talkative warrior. "Is he dead in there?"

"I don't know. He didn't move."

"Those at Kulal Village said he died beside his camel. Somebody must have moved him."

Leslie pulled back the flap for another look and stiffened. Firingin's eyes were open and fearful.

"Firingin!"

His mouth worked.

"We came to..."

Both warriors crowded close, looking over her shoulder. She turned to them. "Bring some water from the camel's carrier. And a cloth. Boil some of the water so I can wash off the blood."

The warriors left.

"We thought you were dead," she said to Firingin. "We..." She started to cry. The anger she'd felt earlier had melted. She saw him, hurt, perhaps dying, and she was overcome with love for this man who had risked everything for her.

Eric pulled at Leslie, and she crawled into the tent and sat down. The talkative warrior leaned in with water and a cloth.

"Try to give him a drink," she ordered.

The warrior tried, but Firingin choked on the offering. "Pour some on the cloth and maybe he'll suck a little." She gingerly pulled aside the blood soaked sleeve of Firingin's robe and saw the wound.

"It's a flesh wound, I believe. Bring more rags and the hot water as soon it's ready. I'll need..."

Firingin touched her. "You are here?" he said.

She smiled. "Yes, we are here."

His eyes closed.

"Drink," she told Firingin. "You've lost a lot of blood so..."

His voice cracked with the words: "Jeidid is dead."

She held up a hand. "Yes, we know about Jeidid."

Firingin's eyes closed. One of the warriors gave the cloth a squeeze over Firingin's dry lips. Water ran down the side of his face.

"The rifle," he rasped, "It killed him."

The effort of speaking seemed too much. He closed his eyes again.

Leslie looked at the warrior. "What do you think he means by that?"

The warrior shook his head.

"Firingin doesn't know how to shoot a rifle," she said.

The warrior held up a hand. "He learned shooting from the one named Jaisut."

"He did?"

Firingin's voice came weakly. "I did not shoot Jeidid. It was the rifle that killed him."

"The rifle killed him," Leslie repeated. "The one that's all splintered to pieces, you mean?"

Firingin gurgled a yes.

"And the people of Kulal have been told that you shot him..."

Firingin said nothing.

Leslie looked at the warrior. "I think that is a lie that can cause a lot of trouble between Kulal Village and people who live with Jeiso."

The warrior nodded.

"You must go back to Kulal Village," she said to the warrior. "Take the rifle with you and show those who told the lie what you found. Tell them we will go to the police with the rifle if they don't tell their elders what really happened. When the elders have heard the truth, you must return and bring the rifle with you."

The warrior nodded and turned to go.

"Eat something before you leave," she said. "There is food on the camel. Go alone and on foot. We will wait for you here. After you return and Firingin is well enough, we will start the trip south."

The warrior left, and Leslie heard him talking in rapid Rendille to his companion.

Eric had finished, and Leslie laid him down beside her.

She held the water gourd carefully to Firingin's lips. His eyelids moved, and he drank for the first time.

When he finished, she told him of going to Hedaidile Village and her plans to clear his name and reverse her marriage to Jeidid.

Firingin smiled, and she told him that she loved him.

He smiled again.

Three days later, the warrior returned and presented Leslie with a talisman, a carved stone from Jesu, the acting head of Kulal Village.

"He says this good luck token will be a symbol of the peace that now remains between his people and the clans of Hedaidile," announced the warrior, and Leslie thanked him for his valuable services.

The group stayed five days longer at the oasis, and with Firingin strong for the walking, it started toward Jeiso's village.

The stops were many at first, and Firingin talked to Leslie about many things. He told of the great wealth his grandfather had bestowed upon him and haltingly said strange words about a woman named Jessina whom he proclaimed he would never marry.

Leslie said nothing but wondered if he meant the widow of his lost cousin, a woman who had once shown a romantic interest in Firingin.

Firingin spoke of the jeweled knife and his grandfather's request that it be retrieved from its hiding place in the desert and be placed with the old one's body at his funeral.

"He wants me to do this thing," said Firingin, "but he has not yet shown me where the knife lies buried."

Again, Leslie had no comment.

She spoke of her plans to go to the police, but Firingin seemed reticent.

"Everyone has a right to defend themselves," she explained, "and the police are certain to realize your innocence and give up their searching if I tell them that you were trying to return me when the soldier attacked you."

Firingin replied that the police were already not searching because they thought him dead. She answered that she would think more about her plan, but it was always better to clear your name if you could.

After a week, the one-camel caravan arrived at Hedaidile Village. The greeting was joyous, and Jeiso immediately ordered a feast of celebration. Leslie renewed her friendship with Wambila, and together they talked of resurrecting the school.

Firingin became the leader of caravans and his wealth grew with each trip he took. On one expedition to Kargi, Leslie went along and then rode the bus to Marsabit.

She met with Chief-Inspector Wanjau, but when she tried to explain Firingin's lack of guilt, the chief-inspector said the case was closed and would remain that way as far as he was concerned. The chief-inspector asked her if she now wished to return to America. She said that she had a husband and a child and had no desire to leave. He dismissed her, and she went to the government offices where she found that she was no longer listed as a wife to Jeidid Wambile.

"Widows of a deceased man are not considered wives," said the clerk who then gave her a look she might have used on one of her least accomplished students.

With the mention of wives, Leslie thought briefly of Deelia and hoped she might see the young woman again some time.

She then asked the clerk to check on Eric's adoption, and after a few minutes of searching though a book with worn edges on its cover, he told her no such adoption had ever been processed.

Leslie returned to the village, and her life became all she'd hoped it would be. Times were often hard for Jeiso's people, but Leslie saw graduates from her school go on to the secondary institutions of Kenya and become star pupils. One of Wambila's sons even went to Nairobi where he attended Jomo Kenyatta University.

After Jeiso's passing and the funeral with the jeweled knife placed in the folds of the old one's robe, Firingin became the village head elder, one of the few in the region with just one wife. Leslie had no more children, but Eric grew tall and strong, and she dreamed of the day when she might take him and his father on a visit to America.

\#   \#   \#